Sri Aurobindo

the
story
of
his life

Sri Aurobindo Ashram
Pondicherry

Sri Aurobindo: the story of his life
(adapted from the Gujarati *Sri Aravindayan*)

First Edition: August 15, 1972
Reprinted: 1974
Second Edition: 1983
Fifth Impression 2001

ISBN 81-7058-079-X

Published by Sri Aurobindo Ashram Publication Department
Printed at Sri Aurobindo Ashram Press, Pondicherry
PRINTED IN INDIA

dedicated to the Mother

"...every symbol was a reality

And brought the Presence which had given it Life."

— *Savitri*

Sri Aurobindo, 1918-20

August 15, 1972
was
the Birth Centenary of Sri Aurobindo
the twenty-fifth anniversary of Free India.
On this day we celebrated
two important events
in the history of the world:
Free India was born on August 15, 1947
Sri Aurobindo was born on August 15, 1872.
Is it strange that these two events should have fallen on the same day?
Yes, strange, and yet not so strange.
It was to Sri Aurobindo when he was in jail
that the Voice of Krishna had said:
"I am raising up this nation to send forth my word...
it is for the world... that they arise...
I am giving them freedom for the service of the world."
As we remember this, the great phrase of the Gita
rings in our ears:
"...I am born from age to age."
August 15, 1947,
Sri Aurobindo said,
"marks... the beginning of a new age....
"We can make it an important date in a new age
opening for the whole world."
That these two events fell on the same day
was surely "the sanction and seal of the Divine"
upon the work of
SRI AUROBINDO.
And so it was, because of its vast significance,
that we celebrated that day,
August 15, 1972.
And year after year
in what better way could we continue to remember it,
Children,
than by hearing the story of his life?

CHAPTER ONE

CHILDHOOD

We begin more than a hundred years ago, in 1869.
There lived, then, in Bengal,
a young doctor,
a very good-hearted and generous man.
Having qualified at the Calcutta Medical College
he went to England for a higher degree.
This was in the days
when to sail the seas
was considered in India a great crime.
The guilty voyager was boycotted, cast out of society.
This doctor was one of those few defiant heroes
who went abroad – headstrong indeed!
Two years later he returned to Calcutta
with an English M.D. degree
and, from top to toe an Englishman –
in dress, in manners, in all the ways of life.
He worked as a Civil Surgeon
at Khulna and Rangpur,
towns in what is now known as Bangla Desh.
His name was Dr. Krishnadhan Ghose.
At the age of nineteen he had married
Swarnalata,
a most beautiful lady,
so fair, that her English friends called her
The Rose of Rangpur.
She was the daughter of Rajnarayan Bose of Devghar.

A strange fancy!

After his return from England
Dr. Ghose developed a strange fancy,

1

almost a mania:
One must live entirely as the English do,
everything must be done in English fashion.
He became so English that he did not like anything Indian:
neither Indian ways of life nor Indian education.
Nor did he believe in God.
He thought everything Indian was bad;
everything English made him glad!
Nothing Indian pleased him, nothing.
That was all.
This bee in his bonnet buzzed and buzzed...
    what could be said?...
And, indeed,
he was not alone in this:
    the times were such
    the whole age thought thus.
The poets of the day openly sang
(while India suffered under British rule, if you please,)
    "Rejoice, O Hindustan!"
Speaking of his father in a passing comment,
Sri Aurobindo once said:
    "My father was a tremendous atheist."
This tremendous atheist, Krishnadhan,
and his wife Swarnalata
had five children:
Benoybhusan, Manmohan,
    Aravinda,
    Sarojini, Barindra.

His name

The third child was Sri Aurobindo,
    born on August 15, 1872.
    His pet name was "Auro".
    Aravind means lotus:
    symbol of beauty, symbol of divinity.

2

And indeed he was lovely as a lotus,
    delicate, gentle,
    very shy. Everybody's favourite.
His speech was – silence,
wondrous the lustre of his eyes,
as though the child remembered "inly, a far home".

Beginning of education

When he was five, the problem of Auro's education arose.
It was impossible to send him to a Bengali national school!
You remember Dr. Ghose's strange fancies?
So, Benoy, Manmohan and Aravinda
were all packed off to Darjeeling.
There was a special school for English children there,
where they would learn only English,
grow up with English children, imbibe only English ways,
not glimpse even a shadow of Aryan culture.
And the result?
Auro
did not know his mother-tongue, Bengali,
did not know Indian culture
nor Indian thought nor Indian ways.

After two years' training in Darjeeling,
the parents took the three boys to England
and left them there for further education.
Auro was then only seven,
and thus, from his very childhood
he was a stranger
to the land of his birth,
to his mother-tongue,
to the life-giving culture of his motherland,
– far, very far apart, lost, alone.
And this in the golden prime of life,
    his youthful student days.

3

The three brothers were left
with an English clergyman and his wife,
with strict instructions
that they should not be allowed
to meet any Indian,
or know anything about India,
or about Indian culture.
They should become accomplished Englishmen:
   this was always to be kept in mind.
And so, at least outwardly, it was amidst
   a fully English setting
    that Auro's education began...

CHAPTER TWO

STUDIES: IN ENGLAND

At Manchester

Now meet Aurobindo in Manchester,
at the Drewetts'.
How and what is he studying?
Mr. Drewett was a clergyman
and he taught Auro English and Latin at home.
His wife taught him arithmetic, history, geography and French,
also at home.
So Auro did not need to go to school at all.
What fun! you would say.
But Auro took delight in altogether other things:
all his spare time he used in reading.
Reading, reading... all the time, reading!
The Bible,
the poets Shelley and Keats,
all of Shakespeare's works.
He travelled to his heart's content
in the realms of gold of European literature.

Mr. Drewett's mother lived with them for some time.
This old lady loved Auro very much
and as she was a fervent Christian,
she wanted to convert him to Christianity.
She grew anxious: such a fine boy, indeed,
his soul must be saved!
And for this, he must become a Christian.
Auro had no inclinations towards Christianity,
but how could the old lady rest in peace?
One day she went to attend
a meeting of priests in Cumberland.
She took Auro with her, but

5

she did not tell him why.
Prayers were said. The work was over,
the gathering began to disperse.
Only a few of the devout remained.
The boy was feeling completely bored.
Then along came a priest
and asked Auro a few questions.
Little Auro, shy as he was,
answered them briefly;
then all present there shouted:
"He is saved! He is saved!"
What happened thereafter we shall recount
    in Sri Aurobindo's own words:
        "Then the priest came to me and asked me to pray. I was
        not in the habit of praying. But somehow I did it in the
        manner in which children recite their prayers before going
        to sleep in order to keep up an appearance."
The old lady then took him from church to church.
He felt tired. But what could he do?
At last, back home in Manchester, he escaped
from this salvation-fancy!

From 1879 to 1892
Aurobindo spent fourteen years in England:
(fourteen years; they bring to our Indian mind
the fourteen years of Rama's appointed exile in the forest.
    What a coincidence!)
five years at Manchester,
seven in London, two in Cambridge and London.

While the three brothers were at Manchester
their father generally used to send the expenses:
£360 per year for the three of them.
This came to just ten pounds a month for each boy,
but still the five years at Manchester
passed fairly easily....

6

London

And Aurobindo went to London.
It was here that the difficulties began.
Why? How? you would ask.
The reason is almost unbelievable today.
His father, Dr. Krishnadhan, was a generous man.
Nay, not merely generous, extremely large-hearted.
If he saw the poor
his heart melted
with pity, with tenderness, with compassion.
Whatever they asked for, he gave,
and in giving, never hesitated, never thought,
    never looked back.
So it was that he could save nothing,
    and had often nothing to send to his sons.
Of the consequences, he did not think.
In his big Government job
he served the people of Rangpur, Khulna,
and wherever else he lived,
worked for them, cared for them,
spent his own money lavishly on them.
In all that wide area
he was well loved, well known.
But,
many a time no money came
for his sons.
Thousands of miles away
his children suffered from poverty and want.

At London Aurobindo was admitted to St. Paul's.
The head-master of the school,
Dr. Walker, was a fine teacher.
He could immediately recognise
    a bright, clever student,
and took great interest in him –
a special personal interest.

7

He would give him special training
and push him up rapidly
so as not to waste his time
with the slow heads.
And he would never forget so clever a boy.
He noticed Aurobindo at once,
    saw that his Latin was brilliant,
    but Greek a little weak.
He coached him thoroughly in that,
saw his capacity in other subjects,
and let him skip several classes.
All his abilities found their flowering:
    he took part in discussions,
    gave talks and lectures,
    shone in all things.
In these five years at St. Paul's
he read much classical literature.
He won the Butterworth prize for literature
    and the Bedford prize for history.

Difficulties! difficulties!
Residence in London:
one would think it must be
endless delight!
The three brothers must be feasting
    and revelling,
having a wonderful time.

But, no...
not at all.
Rather the very opposite.
The fourteen-year-old Auro
had a most difficult time.
A most difficult time,
a time of trial and test:
on all sides difficulties,
fearful poverty, want.

They had nothing to eat,
so the eldest brother, Benoybhusan,
took a job, even while studying.
He earned five shillings a week,
£1 per month.
Just imagine!
  – about eighteen rupees.
And for this he had to toil hard
  while yet a student.
What difficult circumstances!

Two years, specially, passed in great hardship.
There was not enough to eat,
for there was hardly any money.
Do you want to know what the boy Auro
ate every day?
In the morning: a cup of tea and a slice or two of bread.
Afternoon: only a cup of tea.
Evening: a penny sausage or a sandwich.
No hearty dinner for two long years!
  And yet, no discontent,
  no complaint.
One-pointedly, with great concentration,
he went on studying,
  studying.

England is of course quite a cold country,
But its winter?...
It just snows and snows!
Such a biting, freezing cold,
you shiver even to imagine it.
Everybody needs an overcoat at least;
but Aurobindo had neither an overcoat,
nor at home a fire
to warm himself.
Not a room of his own to sleep in either.

9

And yet,
not a word of complaint.
He just went on studying
and alongside, reading
all sorts of other things:
    English Poetry and fiction,
    French Literature,
    the History of Europe, a little briefly;
    of Italian, German, Spanish
    he learnt a little also.
His school studies did not take much time,
    so he read a lot of other works.
(Teachers usually do not like
    a student's concentration so disturbed!)
But Aurobindo surprised all
    by carrying away all the prizes
    for the Classics.

In extreme want

And how utterly grave was the poverty,
    do you want to know?
Let us hear about it in Sri Aurobindo's own words in his letter
to the Secretary of State for India:
    "I was sent over to England when seven years of age, with
    my two elder brothers, and for the last eight years we have
    been thrown on our own resources without any English
    friend to help or advise us. Our father, Dr. K.D. Ghose of
    Khulna, has been unable to provide the three of us with
    sufficient [money] for the most necessary wants and we
    have long been in an embarrassed position."

All the three brothers were short of money,
but Aurobindo was a candidate for the I.C.S.
and later used to get a stipend for that.
He had also won a scholarship at St. Paul's.

10

And so from these he used to try to support
his two brothers.
But he had nothing left for himself.
(What love, what generosity and heroism!)
A Senior Fellow and tutor at Cambridge,
G.W. Prothero,
who knew Aurobindo's hardships intimately,
writes thus of him:

> "...the man has not only ability but character. He has had a
> very hard and anxious time of it for the last two years.
> Supplies from home have almost entirely failed, and he has
> had to keep his two brothers as well as himself, and yet his
> courage and perseverance have never failed.... His whole
> way of life... was simple and penurious in the extreme...."

How very interesting is this frank description
from an Englishman of understanding.

Poetry!

Amidst all these difficulties,
    without enough to eat or wear,
Aurobindo steadily goes on studying,
one-pointedly,
and along with that composes poetry.
Yes, poetry!
And in English, Greek and Latin.
He started writing poetry when he was about sixteen,
and wrote it throughout his life.
Savitri, the great epic, crowns his work.
You will hear more about it a little later.

11

CHAPTER THREE

LOVE OF THE MOTHERLAND

Seeds of Patriotism

We would surely wonder
how, in one who had spent
all his childhood and youth
in the glamour of the West,
amidst western ways of life,
and European studies,
and European culture,
how, in him could awake
so deep a love of India, his motherland.
Where were its seeds?
When were they sown?
And how? By whom?
How powerful must have been the awakening,
that this youth, so gentle, shy, silent, wise,
unhesitatingly leaped into the utmost danger
and was ready to sacrifice his very life
for his country, his country's freedom.
The answer is most interesting – and
      unexpected.
It was his own father who sowed the seeds.
Can you believe it? And yet, it is true.
Dr. Krishnadhan, though quite anglicised in all his ways,
had a deep-seated love of his land.
Even as great as his generosity
was his patriotism – or greater.
Deep within him this love ever burnt.
The British Government of those days
was heartless, oppressive, cruel,
unjust to Indians, ignorant, unwise.
Dr. Ghose could not bear to see Indians

12

maltreated by the British.
Though he liked many Englishmen and their ways,
he denounced the Government.
Whenever he wrote to his sons in England
he told them of the Government injustice,
its high-handed ways towards Indians,
its terrible oppression.
He began sending newspaper cuttings,
marking passages describing this ill-treatment.
And Aurobindo slowly took in the whole situation;
    and what was the effect?
All his thoughts and feelings turned
towards the liberation of India...
– yes, even when he was still on England's soil.
And while yet in his teens,
he took a firm decision
to liberate his country.
It was in this strange way
that the beautiful seeds of patriotism
were sown in his heart.
And how deep and far the roots went
we soon shall see.

An experience

For the moment, let us glance at a "small" experience:
Someone once asked Sri Aurobindo
whether he had any kind of "yogic" experience
in his early years.
In reply he recalled an incident at Darjeeling:
   "I was lying down one day when I saw suddenly a great
   darkness rushing into me and enveloping me and the whole
   universe. After that I had a great *tamas* always hanging on
   to me all along my stay in England. I believe that darkness
   had something to do with the *tamas* that came upon me. It
   left me only when I was coming back to India."

13

An "impression"

Sri Aurobindo himself also spoke of another vivid impression:
   "At the age of eleven he had already received a strong
   impression that a period of general upheaval and great
   revolutionary changes was coming in the world and he
   himself was destined to play a part in it."
This was not a mere idea
but a kind of inner feeling –
and this feeling went on growing strongly –
that he was meant to do some great work,
to fulfil some great purpose.

There was a second "inner" change.
He was then about thirteen.
He kept on feeling that he was selfish,
and felt from within that
he must give up all selfishness.
He resolved to give it up,
and commenced the practice.
And from then onwards
his life was completely changed:
thereafter, all the knowledge in the mind
had to be immediately put into practice –
this was a rule with him even from childhood.
This is the very master-key of his life:
nothing, not the least thing, should be left out,
all must be taken up, purified, transformed.

At Cambridge

From 1890 to 1892:
at King's College, Cambridge.
In two years he passed the First Part of the Classical Tripos,
for which others take three years generally.
And he passed in the First Class.

14

Yet the rule was that the B.A. degree
was conferred only after three years.
But Sri Aurobindo did not care for the degree:
the knowledge is not broken and lost.
Two years were enough there:
    he wanted to get back to India, now.

The "Majlis" and "Lotus and Dagger"

At Cambridge
the Indian students had formed a *Majlis*, a revolutionary society.
Aurobindo joined it, became its secretary,
took a leading part in it.
He delivered many revolutionary speeches,
couched in the strongest language,
filled with a fiery love for his country.
The India Office took note of this,
recorded it as a black mark against him,
and ever since, the Government kept a watch on him.
Apart from this there was the Indian students' secret society
of which also he became a member.
It had a romantic name: "Lotus and Dagger".
Every member had to take a vow
to dedicate his entire life to the liberation of India.
This society, however, had but one meeting in London
    just before Aurobindo left for India.

I.C.S.

At Cambridge he obtained prizes for Greek and Latin verse.
He passed the I.C.S., but felt no call for it,
for he knew it meant serving under the yoke of the
                              British Government:
he did not want to be a slave of this government
which he was already criticising so severely.
He resolved not to be trapped

15

by the "Service", to escape that bondage.
And so....
He managed to get himself disqualified for the riding test.
Again and again chances were given,
but he would not present himself in time!
For, should he have passed, he would have had to join;
he could not have disappointed his father by rejecting
the Service.
About his early life Sri Aurobindo says:
"...I was a great coward. Nobody could have imagined that later on I could face the gallows or carry on a revolutionary movement. In my case it was all human imperfection with which I had to start,* feel all the difficulties before embodying the Divine Consciousness."
When asked why he appeared for the I.C.S. at all,
he said:
"I appeared for the I.C.S. because my father wanted it and I was too young to understand. Later, I found out what sort of work it was and I had a disgust for the administrator's life and no interest in administrative work. My interest was in poetry and literature and study of languages and patriotic action."

We can now understand what happened:
this youth, so fond of poetry, literature,
so drunk with the love of the Motherland,
how could he fall into the snare of the I.C.S.?
He got a good opportunity in the Riding Test:
he had been given a last chance,
but deliberately missing his train,
wandering through the London streets,
he went late, too late!

* It is interesting to compare this account with Sri Aurobindo's description of the truth behind:

Coercing my godhead I have come down
Here on this sordid earth,
Ignorant, labouring, human grown
Twixt the gates of death and birth.

16

Leisurely he walked back home
as though nothing had happened.
He told his eldest brother, Benoy, with a smile,
"I am chucked out."
His brother said with a philosophical air,
"What does it matter?
Come, let us play cards."
So they were seated, quietly, as though all were well,
when later in the evening, Manmohan dropped in.
But he, on learning about the I.C.S. rejection,
set up a howl as though the heavens had fallen!
However he calmed down and after that all the three
sat smoking and playing cards.

The Gaekwad

And now what next?
He had escaped the I.C.S. bondage,
but now...?
He had to do something, he had to earn money,
he had nothing to live on.
Then they thought of asking a friend of their father's,
James Cotton, whom both Benoy and Aurobindo knew well.
He was a very kind man, took much interest in them,
and would surely help.
Through him was arranged a meeting
with the Maharaja of Baroda, Sir Sayaji Rao.
The Gaekwad was a good judge of men and things,
he travelled much and picked up the best everywhere
and brought it home.
He immediately recognised the worth of this resplendent youth,
and engaged him there and then –
(indeed like a real business man) –
for a mere Rs.200 a month.
What a meagre salary!
But it was others who arranged everything for Aurobindo – he

17

himself had no experience of life and did not bother about
these things.
The Gaekwad, it seems, used to boast afterwards
that he had obtained an I.C.S. man for a paltry Rs.200!
– nay, was it not a very Kohinoor for Rs.200?

The last sum due on passing the final I.C.S.
was applied for and obtained: £ 150.
Aurobindo paid off all debts,
bought his passage
and in February 1893 returned to India
by the *S. S. Carthage*.

A sad incident

In a letter dated December 2, 1890,
Dr. Krishnadhan wrote to his brother-in-law:
   "The three sons I have produced, I have made giants of
   them... Auro, I hope, will yet glorify his country by a
   brilliant administration. I shall not live to see it, but
   remember this letter if you do...."
This son, Auro, of whom he had such great expectations,
is now, after fourteen years of painful separation,
back on his way to India.
Consider how eager the father must be to see him,
to meet him, embrace him.
How anxiously he was awaiting his son... and...
and...
the unexpected happened!
Just one small (small?) mistake, and...
This is what happened:
Messrs. Grindlay & Co., Dr. Ghose's bankers in London,
informed him that Aurobindo had set sail
by a certain steamer for India.
They mentioned a wrong name, not the *S. S. Carthage*.
And strangely enough

18

that very steamer sank off the coast of Portugal.
The accident was disastrous,
no one, nothing was saved.
The news flashed forth in paper and paper,
and Dr. Ghose too came to know.
Alas! the steamer that had Aurobindo on board
(so he thought)
was gone, gone beyond all hope.
He received a terrible shock indeed:
he thought his dearest, most precious Auro was drowned.
And his heart broke.
He died repeating Aurobindo's name.

INDIA

But Aurobindo reached India safely by the *Carthage*.
This was at the beginning of February 1893.
He was nearly twenty-one.
He felt on the one hand the deep sorrow of his father's loss,
on the other, the great joy of being back
in his Motherland.
How strange indeed are the ways of Fate!

An experience

February 1893: the first week.
The *Carthage* anchored in Bombay harbour.
This brilliant youth, aflame with love for his country,
– after fourteen years' "exile",
fourteen years' *tapas* in a foreign land, –
set foot once more
on the purifying Indian soil,
"richly-watered, richly-fruited".
He stepped ashore –
and lo, what a marvellous experience!
PEACE!

19

A vast calm descended upon him
with his first step on Apollo Bunder,
a deep peace
which surrounded him
and remained for long months afterwards.
One of his first spiritual experiences,
it came all unasked;
after it came many and many another,
infinite and vast and varied.
This was but the auspicious beginning
of his long spiritual life.

20

CHAPTER FOUR

AT BARODA

After fourteen years abroad, in a foreign land,
when a man returns home
he feels like meeting his family, his friends, his loved ones,
feels like spending some time in leisurely enjoyment.
But the young Aurobindo, what did he do?
Nothing of that kind:
Pleasure and ease never crossed his mind.
He joined the service of the Gaekwad immediately.
It was the 8th of February, 1893.
Sayaji Rao who had secured a "Civilian" for Rs.200 a month
gave him all sorts of jobs,
in all sorts of places:
Land Settlement Department
Stamps Office
Central Revenue Office
The Secretariat
The Vahivatdar's Office.
Then he became (informally at first)
Professor of French at Baroda College,
later also Professor of English,
finally Vice-Principal.
And at the same time, along with his usual work,
the Maharaja used to call him
to write important letters and drafts that needed
careful wording,
to prepare his public speeches for him,
draw up documents
and for several other jobs of a literary or educational type.
Though not his Private Secretary
he used to do much personal work for him unofficially –
without complaint, with great diligence, great love.

21

It was his very nature
to do his work with concentration, with love and joy,
bringing it to its perfection.

Yet he neither flattered the Maharaja nor ever feared him.
Of his straightforwardness an instance is narrated
in a book of Reminiscences
of a Maharashtrian writer. He says,

"Sri Aurobindo and I often used to meet at Sayaji Rao's.
Often he used to write the speeches for the Maharaja.

"Once the Maharaja had to speak at a Social Conference.
Sri Aurobindo prepared the speech and we three read it
together. Then the Maharaja said, "Arvindbabu, could you
not make the speech a little simpler? It is so good that
nobody will believe it is mine!"

"Sri Aurobindo answered: 'Why unnecessarily change it?
Do you suppose, Saheb, that if it is a little simpler people
will take it as yours? Whether it is good or bad, they will say
that the Maharaja always has his speeches written out for
him. The main thing is to see whether the thoughts there are
yours or not'."

There is another interesting remark about Sri Aurobindo in
the same book:

"He spoke very little. When asked a question he usually
used to say just 'Yes' or 'No' and stop – would not speak
further. There was something yogic about him."

Patriotic activities

He had been only six months in India
but he had studied everything about the political movement,
the conditions of the country,
the patriotic activities,
the leaders, their ways, their ideas.
And just then
an old Cambridge friend, one of the members of the *Majlis*,

22

K.G. Deshpande, who was editor of the *Indu Prakash*,
invited Sri Aurobindo to write a series of articles for his paper.
He must have remembered the *Majlis*,
Aurobindo's fiery, powerful revolutionary speeches,
ringing with patriotism, with the love of the Motherland,
so touching, so soul-moving.
Hoping to get something new and vigorous from his pen
he asked him to write about the Indian National Congress of
those days,
its leaders, their aims, the political progress.
Seizing the opportunity, Arvindbabu contributed his views
in no uncertain terms;
and thus began
his first political activity.

"New Lamps for Old"

It was under this very suggestive title that
Sri Aurobindo wrote these articles,
full of keen observations,
criticising strongly the prevailing moderate policy
of the Congress
and trying to awaken the nation
to the ideas of the future.
He did not give his name, for he was in the Baroda Service and
could not write openly on political matters.
Hardly had the first two articles been published
than they created a sensation,
a wild furore in political circles.
The Congress leaders started wondering:
Who could be the writer?
There was an enquiry,
but nobody could find out.
Ranade, the famous Maratha leader
warned the proprietor of the paper that if this went on
he would be prosecuted for sedition.

23

What could there have been in those articles
to have scared them all so much?
You have to read them all to find out,
but still, here are the chief points:

1. "I say of the Congress, then, this – that its aims are
   mistaken, that the spirit in which it proceeds towards their
   accomplishment is not a spirit of sincerity and whole-
   heartedness,... the methods... are not the right methods,
   the leaders... are not the right sort of men to be leaders;
   ...we are at present the blind led, if not by the blind, at any
   rate by the one-eyed."

2. "...by reflection or instinct to get a clear insight into our
   position and by dexterity to make the most of it, that is the
   whole secret of politics, and that is just what we have failed
   to do."

3. "We lose in sincerity which is another name for strength."

This series of articles reveals the twenty-one year old

Aurobindo wonderfully:

His subtle power of thought,
his marvellous all-compassing grasp of things,
his mastery of the language,
his utter sincerity, his courage,
burning patriotism, absolute selflessness.

When he was told to write in a modified tone,
he reluctantly consented,
began writing on the philosophy of politics
instead of the practical side,
then lost interest and stopped.

At the end of the year, during the holidays, he went to Bengal
for the first time and met his mother, his sister, his younger
brother Barin and other relatives. Sarojini, his sister, records
her impression:
"a very delicate face, long hair,...
– he was extremely shy!"

24

Ranade

On his way back to Baroda
at Bombay he met the great leader, Ranade,
who had been so alarmed by the *Indu Prakash* articles.
In a half-hour interview, he advised Arvindbabu thus:
    "Instead of attacking and criticising the Congress violently,
    it would be better to try something like jail reform! That
    work would be more useful."
(Many years later, in the dark horrible cell of Alipore jail,
Sri Aurobindo vividly recalled these words.)
This was the turn of thought of the Moderate leaders
                                               of the time.
How could they tolerate the fiery speech of Arvindbabu?
It would surely burn them!

Studies

During this period Aurobindo read much,
thought much, studied deeply –
this was the time of preparation for his future activities.
His first book of poetry, *Songs to Myrtilla* was published.
Then *Love and Death* was rapidly written, and much other
                                               verse,
and we know that the earliest version of *Savitri*
                                   was begun in this period.
He read Homer, Dante, Vyasa, Kalidas, Bhavabhuti, and
many, many other great writers.
He learnt Sanskrit all by himself,
also Gujarati and Marathi which were used in Baroda State.
He had started learning Bengali in England
but now called the well-known author Dinendra Kumar Roy
to help him perfect his knowledge of the language
and accustom him to conversation in Bengali.
He lived with Sri Aurobindo for nearly two years
as his companion.

25

He saw books arrive by railway parcels,
packed in huge cases;
heaps and heaps of them!
English, French, German, Italian, Greek, Latin,
books in all languages –
which Sri Aurobindo read up as fast as they came.
When he went for his holidays
he would take trunkfuls of books.
His luggage was a mobile library.

Fancy and Reality

Dinendra Kumar's first impression of Sri Aurobindo
is both amusing and striking.
He says, "Before I met Aurobindo I had imagined him as a
tall, stalwart figure, dressed from head to foot in immaculate
European style, bespectacled, with a stern piercing look and
an affected accent, quick-tempered, intolerant.
"Frankly I was a little disappointed when I saw him!
"Here was a shy, dark youth, his gentle eyes filled with dream,
his long, soft, shining hair, parted in the middle and flowing
down to the neck; he was dressed in a thick coarse dhoti and
close-fitting Indian jacket and wore old-fashioned slippers
with upturned toes. 'Is this Srijut Aurobindo Ghose?' I asked
myself. 'Is this the living image of the great scholar of Greek
and French and Latin? Who could have imagined it, believed
it?' "
Dinendra Roy continues:
"In the short time I lived with him
I saw clearly that his heart was pure and unworldly.
He smiled and laughed like a child, frankly, gently.
The corners of his lips expressed a power of inflexible will,
yet in his heart
there was not a trace of worldly ambition
or of any human selfish motives.
He had but one deep yearning,

26

rare even among the gods –
to give his whole being as a sacrifice
that humanity's sufferings may disappear....
I used to stay with him
and as I gradually came to know him closely
I felt more and more that this man
was not a man of this earth,
he was a God come down from his heavens
as though by some curse*...
...Always I saw that he lived like a real self-denying sannyasin,
austere in self-discipline,
but feeling deeply others' pain....
He had but one aim in life, it seemed to me:
to gather knowledge,
and for its realisation
in the very midst of the world's noise and bustle
he lived the hard life of a *tapasvi*...
I never saw him angry...."

Denials!

Not angry, yes.
But this did not mean
that if anything was wrong
he would put up with it.
See what he did once:
The Maharaja had issued a Circular to the effect that all
officers should go to work on Saturdays and Sundays also.
All, however unwillingly, went.
Arvindbabu did not.
That meant insulting the Maharaja's Circular!

* Not by a curse. Sri Aurobindo gives the reason in his poem *A God's Labour*:

> He who would bring the heavens here
> Must descend himself into clay,
> And the burden of earthly nature bear
> And tread the dolorous way.

Sayaji Rao heard about it and, furious,
resolved to fine him heavily.
The news was carried to Arvindbabu.
Calm, firm, unmoved, all he said was:
'Let him fine me as much as he likes,
I shan't go!'
The Maharaja dropped the idea, as though nothing had
happened, for he now knew that Arvindbabu could not be
made to submit.
Sriyut Roy has another reminiscence:
"At times, in the evenings or late afternoons
a horseman would come from the Palace
with a message for Arvindbabu:
" 'The Maharaja will be pleased if you will dine with him
tonight' or 'Will you let the Maharaja know at what time it
would be convenient for you to meet him?' Well, I saw that if
he was short of time he would refuse the invitation! Many
important people longed for just one meeting with the
Maharaja, spent months dancing attendance on him to obtain
it, and here was a mere teacher who considered his own work
more important than the Maharaja's favour!"
Dinendra Kumar writes further:
"He was alone, he did not know what it was to run after
pleasures, knew no luxury, no extravagance; he never spent
even a pie in the wrong way, and yet at the end of the month
he had nothing left!"

Money matters

Talking about money, there is a very interesting account in
the Reminiscences of a Baroda advocate, Sriyut Patkar, who
knew Sri Aurobindo quite intimately. He says:

"Another thing I observed about him was the total absence
of love for money. He used to get the lump-sum of three
months' pay in a bag which he emptied in a tray lying on his
table. He never bothered to keep money in a safe-box under

lock and key. He did not keep an account of what he spent. One day I casually asked him why he was keeping money like that. He laughed and then replied: 'Well, it is a proof that we are living in the midst of honest and good people.' – 'But you never keep an account which may testify to this?' – Then with a serene face he said: 'It is God who keeps the account for me. He gives me as much as I want and keeps the rest to Himself. At any rate he does not keep me in want, then why should I worry?' "
Complete surrender,
an absolute self-giving to God –
without that, how could such words be spoken?
But he used to send money regularly for the maintenance of his mother and for Sarojini's education. The two elder brothers, Benoybhusan and Manmohan were earning well also, but gave no help to the family. When asked about this, Sri Aurobindo used to say: "Dada is in Cooch Bihar State Service and so has to maintain a certain high standard of living. Manmohan is married and marriage is an expensive luxury!"

A wonderful power of concentration

Of his power of concentration, his friend and co-worker in the political field, Charu Chandra Dutt, I.C.S., gives a remarkable instance:

"Once, back from the College, Sri Aurobindo picked up a novel lying close by and began to read it, while some of us were noisily engaged in a game of chess. After about half an hour he put down the book and took a cup of tea. We had often noticed him doing this sort of thing before and were eagerly awaiting an opportunity to test whether he read the books from cover to cover or only glanced through them. So we at once subjected him to a *viva* test. I opened the book at random and read out a line, asking Sri Aurobindo to say what followed. Sri Aurobindo thought for a moment, and then repeated the contents of the page without a mistake!"

No wonder he could read parcels of books in a week's time!

CHAPTER FIVE

THE REVOLUTIONARY

Preparations for Revolutionary Work

1898, 1899
Sri Aurobindo, through the help of his friends,
had Jatin Banerjee, a young Bengali,
enlisted as a trooper in the Baroda Army
to get military training for the revolutionary work.
It was as a U.P. man that he had been enlisted,
for the British Government had prohibited
the enlistment of any Bengali in any army.
After a year's training Sri Aurobindo sent him to Calcutta
with a programme of preparation and action
to get men, means, money, materials,
for revolutionary activities.
He was extremely energetic and capable, formed a first group
which grew rapidly, and entered into relations with other
revolutionaries already at work in Bengal.

Another spiritual experience

In his first year at Baroda,
once Sri Aurobindo was in danger of a carriage accident,
when he had the vision of the Godhead surging up from within,
who was master of the situation and averted the danger.
This was before he knew anything about Yoga or had done
any Sadhana – just like the experience of the vast calm at
Apollo Bunder, his first spiritual experience.
     He describes this incident in a very powerful sonnet entitled
The Godhead.
Here are a few lines from it:

> Above my head a mighty head was seen,
>   A face with the calm of immortality...

Sri Aurobindo at St. Paul's School, London, 1884

Sri Aurobindo in Alipore Jail, 1908

His hair was mingled with the sun and breeze;
　　　　　The world was in His heart and He was I;
　　　I housed in me the Everlasting's peace,
　　　　　The strength of One whose substance cannot die.

1901 is an important year for Sri Aurobindo:
First, the secret preparations of revolutionary groups,
secondly, marriage.
He was twenty-nine then,
his wife, Mrinalini, was fourteen.
The marriage was arranged by a common friend
and celebrated according to Hindu ritual.
As Sri Aurobindo had been to England,
the orthodox raised the question of purificatory rites;
but he flatly refused any expiation,
even as his father had done in his time.
At last there was a proposal from the priests
that he should shave his head!
But when this too was turned down
"an obliging Brahmin priest
satisfied all the requirements of the Shastra
for a monetary consideration!"
It is in his "Letters to Mrinalini" which were meant to be
absolutely private and secret, that we see what was really
going on within him in those days, and his true relation with
his wife. We shall read parts from them a few pages later.

Secret Revolutionary Societies

In 1902 Sri Aurobindo went to Bengal during the vacation.
He practised rifle shooting,
resolved with other friends
to form revolutionary centres in Bengal.
He joined the revolutionaries there
and tried to bring the existing revolutionary groups together.
With a sword and the Gita in his hands

31

he gave this solemn oath:
To secure the freedom of Mother India at any cost,
and not to declare the secret of the Society to anyone.
Other revolutionary societies had been formed in
                                    Maharashtra,
and Sri Aurobindo had joined the Bombay branch already.

About this time he sent his brother Barin
to help Jatin Banerjee in Calcutta.
(It was this Jatin who had been given
military training at Baroda).
Jatin used to work among the educated classes,
Barin with another friend, Abinash,
worked among students.
They organised these young men
and under the cover of sports-groups
for lathi play, fencing, even riding,
prepared them for revolution.
The work spread enormously and finally included
tens of thousands of young men,
and the spirit of revolution
took hold of the young generation.
Sri Aurobindo went over to Bengal again early in 1903,
but was soon called back by the Maharaja
to accompany him to Kashmir.

Another spiritual experience

It was in Kashmir that Sri Aurobindo had, quite unexpectedly,
a third powerful spiritual experience: "the realisation of the
vacant Infinite while walking on the ridge of the Takht-i-
Suleiman." The 'Takht-i-Suleiman' (Throne of Solomon) is a
hill on which there was a temple dedicated to the great
Shankaracharya. Sri Aurobindo describes this experience
vividly in his sonnet *Adwaita*.

32

"Experiences"

People usually believe that
only what we see
what we hear
what we touch
is real, nothing else.
Sri Aurobindo too in his early life
did not believe in 'supernatural' things.
But many experiences gradually showed him their truth.

It was in 1904 that Sri Aurobido started
learning Pranayama from a friend of his
who was a disciple of Swami Brahmanand of Chandod.
He describes the results:

"My own experience is that the brain becomes *prakasha-maya* – full of light. When I was practising *pranayama* I used to do it for five to six hours a day.... The mind worked with great illumination and power. At that time I used to write poetry.... Usually I wrote... about two hundred lines a month. After *pranayama* I could write two hundred lines within half an hour.... I could see an electric energy all around the brain."

Many visions, luminous patterns and figures also came as a result of *pranayama*, but after some time everything stopped. Yet, let us have a glimpse of what was going on within him.

Letters to Mrinalini

A while ago you heard about Sri Aurobindo's letters to Mrinalini. They were meant to be absolutely private, as you know. It was in the most unexpected way that they became known.

When Sri Aurobindo was arrested and sent to jail and there was a police-search for his private papers, these letters were discovered, and produced in Court.
They contain the first statement
of the burning aspiration of his soul,

33

his thirst for God, his intense yearning to see Him,
his passionate love for his Motherland.
Let us read some of the most beautiful passages in them. They
were written in Bengali, but here is a translation.

His three madnesses

In his historical letter dated August 30, 1905,
Sri Aurobindo says:
"I have three madnesses:

"The first is that I firmly believe that whatever virtue,
talent, learning and knowledge and wealth God has given me,
all belong to Him, and that I am entitled to spend only as
much as is needed for the maintenance of the family and on
what is absolutely necessary; whatever remains should be
returned to God...

"The second folly has recently taken hold of me. It is this:
by whatever means I must see God face to face, get His direct
realisation. The religion of today consists in repeating the
name of God every now and again, and in praying to Him in
everybody's presence and in showing to people how religious
one is. I do not want it. If God is there, then there must be a
way of experiencing His existence, of realising His presence.
However hard the path, I am resolved to follow it.... I would
like to take you also along that path.... Anybody can reach
perfection by following it. But it depends on one's choice to
enter the path.

"The third folly is this: Others look upon their country as a
mass of matter, a number of fields, plains, forests, mountains
and rivers, and nothing more. I look upon her as my mother. I
worship and adore her. What would a son do when he sees a
demon sitting upon his mother's chest drinking her life-
blood? Would he sit down quietly to his meals and enjoy
himself?... Or would he rather run to his mother's rescue?

"I know I have the strength to uplift this fallen race. It is not
physical power... but the power of knowledge. The prowess

34

of the Kshatriya is not the only force; there is the fire-power of
the Brahmin, the blazing power of spiritual knowledge. This
is not a new feeling within me, I was born with it, it is in my
very marrow. It is to accomplish this great mission that God
has sent me to the earth...."
It is in this very letter that he says:
"The whole country is at my doors,
seeking for shelter and help...
millions of my brethren
of whom many are dying of starvation....
They must be helped."
He carried "the sorrow of millions in his lonely breast", as he
                                said later in one of his sonnets.
He ends the letter with a tender request:
   "This is the secret I wanted to tell you. Don't breathe a
   word of it to anybody".
It is only in these letters that we have an intimate revelation of
Sri Aurobindo's inmost thoughts and feelings in those days.
After this we have to wait for the Uttarpara Speech to get
another.

   Mrinalinidevi perhaps did not fully understand him, for she
did not follow him. She lived in Calcutta till her death in 1918.
But she received initiation, *diksha*, from the saintly wife of Sri
Ramakrishna, Saradamani Devi, and was very fortunate to
have found so great a spiritual refuge.

Brahmanand

The next year
Sri Aurobindo went with some of his friends
to the Yogi Brahmanand
in his Gangamath at Chandod.
Something special happened:
Brahmanand generally used to keep his eyes closed
when people went for *pranam*.

35

When their party was about to leave, one by one,
they all went to bow before him.
But when Sri Aurobindo did *pranam*,
Brahmanand opened his beautiful eyes
and looked full at him –
as if he saw something extraordinary or
as if he had recognised somebody.

"The Stone Goddess"

Another very illuminating incident also occurred near
Chandod:

Sri Aurobindo went along with some friends to visit a
temple of Kali on the banks of the Narmada. He just strolled
there, for he had no attraction towards image-worship and
was in fact against it. But when he went into the shrine he
found a living presence in the image.
Suddenly he understood the truth behind image-worship.
He speaks of this in one of his letters:

"You stand before a temple of Kali beside a sacred river
and see what? – a sculpture; a gracious piece of architec-
ture; but in a moment mysteriously, unexpectedly there is
instead a Presence, a Power, a Face that looks into yours;
an inner sight in you has regarded the World-Mother".

Sri Aurobindo has also written a beautiful sonnet
about the same experience.
It is called *The Stone Goddess*.
Let us read a stanza or two from it:

In a town of Gods, housed in a little shrine,
    From sculptured limbs the Godhead looked at me, –
A living Presence, deathless and divine,
    A Form that harboured all infinity....

Now veiled with mind she dwells and speaks no word...
Hiding until our soul has seen, has heard
    The secret of her strange embodiment.

36

We see how many spiritual experiences came of themselves to him, with a sudden unexpectedness, before he had even begun Yoga seriously.

Yoga and Politics

For at that time he did not want to practise yoga.
When a friend seeing his natural bent
asked him to do so, he said:
  "A yoga which requires me to give up the world is not for
  me. I have to liberate my country."
He felt that "a solitary salvation leaving the world to its fate"
was not the right thing for him.
"It was the time of country first", as he said later.
But then something happened which showed him that yoga
gives power, and he wanted power to liberate India.

It is a strange story – yet not unusual in India:
Barin, his brother, had caught a violent and clinging hill-
                                                        fever.
He was being treated, but the fever would not go;
just then a Naga Sannyasi happened to come wandering by.
He took a glassful of water,
cut it crosswise with a knife
while chanting a *mantra*,
and asked Barin to drink it.
And almost in a moment the fever left him.
Sri Aurobindo thus had a direct proof of the power of Yoga.
"So when I turned to Yoga", he said much later,
"and resolved to practise it...
I did it in this spirit and with this prayer:
'If Thou art, then Thou knowest my heart...
Thou knowest that I do not ask for Mukti,
I do not ask for anything which others ask for.
I ask only for strength to uplift this nation,

37

I ask only to be allowed to work for this people
whom I love' ..."

Therefore when he did start yoga, there was no conflict or
wavering between yoga and politics, he carried on both
without any opposition between them.
"The Sanatana Dharma, that is Nationalism", he said.

Partition of Bengal – 1905

When the British Government
passed the black act of the Partition of Bengal,
all over India there was a tremendous agitation,
public meetings were held everywhere to protest against it,
there was an outburst of revolt.
The whole nation arose from its slumber,
the cry of 'Swaraj' and 'Swadeshi' spread over the land,
the great Nationalist movement was openly started.

"Bhavani Mandir"

During the Bengal-Partition days a small revolutionary
                                    booklet *Bhavani Mandir*
was circulated throughout the country.
It was written by Sri Aurobindo.
Patriots, lovers of the motherland, must have spiritual
                                            strength, he said.
To prepare them, a plan was worked out in some detail:
A temple was to be built and consecrated
to "the Mother of strength, the Mother of India".
"We will build it... in a high and pure air
steeped in calm and energy."
Here were to be trained "a new order of Karmayogins...
men who have renounced all in order to work for the Mother,"
for the freedom of India.

38

These would be helped by others all over the country
who could sacrifice something for their Motherland.
For "what is our mother-country?
It is not a piece of earth...
It is a mighty Shakti...
The Shakti we call India, Bhavani Bharati,
is the living unity of the shaktis of three hundred
                                        million people...
the energy of God is within us...
It is to India that is reserved the highest
and the most splendid destiny,
the most essential to the future of the human race..."
"Spiritual energy is the source of all other strength.
There are the fathomless fountain-heads, the deep and
                                        inexhaustible sources."
This Infinite Energy is "the Mother of the Universe,
the Mother of the Worlds."
She says:
"For you who are my children of the Sacred Land, Aryabhumi,
made of her clay and reared by her sun and winds,
I am Bhavani Bharati,
Mother India."
It was the call of the Motherland
to all who were young and high-spirited, to all her children,
to worship and serve her with knowledge
in a complete self-giving,
with strength gathered from spiritual living and enlightenment.

Thousands of youths answered the call.

Today also the same call stands, the same call comes.

39

CHAPTER SIX

THE NATIONALIST MOVEMENT

Sri Aurobindo went again to Bengal and this time
plunged deep into political action.

And the next year when the National College was started,
he threw away the Baroda College job of Rs.710 and went to
Calcutta as Principal of the new college for a mere Rs.150.
He wanted to work for the Nation,
and never cared for money, as you know.
A Bengali paper, *Yugantar*, had been started a few months
earlier to preach open revolt and absolute denial of British rule.
Sri Aurobindo wrote several opening articles in the early
numbers, though the editor was his brother, Barin.
It had as its chief writers three of the ablest
young men in Bengal,
and immediately gained an immense influence.
Specially when one of the sub-editors was prosecuted,
and under Sri Aurobindo's orders the *Yugantar*
refused to defend itself in a British Court,
its prestige and influence increased immensely.

"Bande Mataram"

It was during this period that Sri Aurobindo
joined Bepin Chandra Pal
in the editing of *Bande Mataram* ("I bow to the Mother").
He took the opportunity to start the public propaganda
necessary for his revolutionary purpose.
His first work was to declare openly
complete and absolute independence as the aim
of political action in India,
and to insist on this again and again in his journal.
He was the first Indian politician to have the courage to do this,

and he was immediately successful.
The party took up the word "Swaraj"
to express its own ideal of independence,
and it soon spread everywhere.
The journal declared and developed a new political
programme:
non-cooperation, passive resistance, Swadeshi,
boycott, national education, popular arbitration, etc.
Sri Aurobindo wanted to push the whole nation
into an intense and organised political activity.
His idea was to capture the Congress
and make it an instrument of revolutionary action
instead of a centre of timid constitutional agitation
which would only talk and pass tame resolutions.
A central revolutionary body, an extremist party,
was formed, its action being
i) increasing non-cooperation and passive resistance to make
the foreign Government's task difficult or impossible,
ii) creating a universal unrest to wear down repression,
iii) finally, if need be, an open revolt all over the country.
The plan included
boycott of British trade
national schools
arbitration courts of the people
volunteer forces.
Sri Aurobindo wrote a series of articles on Passive Resistance,
and another series developing a political philosophy of
revolution.

He wanted to destroy all the wrong ideas of the Moderate
Party about British justice and benefits bestowed by a foreign
government, their faith in British law courts and in the
ruinous education that was then given.
He stressed the stagnation or slow progress,
the poverty, economic dependence, crippled industries,
all the evil results of a foreign government.
He insisted that even if an alien rule is benevolent

it is no substitute for a free and healthy national life.
The *Bande Mataram* began to circulate throughout India. It
was unique in the influence it exercised in converting the mind
of the people and preparing it for revolution.
Yet the articles were so cleverly written that
it could not be prosecuted.
A British editor complained
that the paper reeked with sedition
which was visible between every line,
yet was so skilfully worded
that no legal action could be taken.

A new spirit was created in the country.
Enthusiasm swept surging everywhere, and
with the cry of "Bande Mataram" ringing on all sides,
men felt it was glorious to be alive
and dare and act together and hope.
The old apathy and timidity were broken,
and a force created which nothing could destroy
and which rose again and again
in wave after wave
carrying India to complete Victory.

> "I saw the mornings of the future rise,
> I heard the voices of an age unborn."

Sri Aurobindo always preferred to remain and act,
even to lead, from behind the scenes.
And, as he says, "History seldom records the things that were
decisive but took place behind the veil; it records the shown
front of the curtain."

He was forced into public view when the Government
prosecuted him as editor of *Bande Mataram*.
But he was acquitted for lack of evidence,
and from that time he became openly
the leader of the Nationalist Party,

the organiser of its policy and strategy.
He led the party at many political conferences,
spoke on the public platform,
addressed large meetings all over the country.

Revolutionary "Diksha"

But what he said at that time in a private interview to
Amarendranath Chatterjee, who became a well-known revo-
lutionary leader later, is most touching.
He gave him the *diksha* (initiation) of Revolution:
"If we want to secure the freedom of the country, we have to
sacrifice everything for it.... Is it so difficult to sacrifice oneself
for the Motherland?... If India does not become free, man
also will not be free.... Surrender yourself to God and in the
name of the Divine Mother get along with the service of India.
That is my *diksha* to you."
Amar said later: "This *diksha* moulded my whole life.
All fear, all attachment left me."

We recall once again Sri Aurobindo's words:
        "The Sanatana Dharma, that is Nationalism."

And so indeed it was for him.
In the midst of the most intense political activity,
whilst he was writing fiery newspaper articles every day,
whilst he was speaking to enormous gatherings
and rousing the whole country to cry for freedom,
something from behind was urging and driving him
deeper and deeper into the spiritual life.
Yoga – yes, now he took to it more seriously,
for he had seen that it could give power,
and he felt that with this power he could free India.
He says humorously,
        "Mine was a side-door entry into the spiritual life."

But his mind was "upon great and distant things."

CHAPTER SEVEN

NIRVANA

A man's outer activities one can describe,
but who can say what goes on within,
who can speak of the life of the spirit?
Sri Aurobindo often said of his life,
"It has not been on the surface for men to see."
Then here we must only recount what he himself has said.

Lele

He had come to a stage when he felt
he wanted further guidance in his *sadhana*.
He spoke of this to Barin, his brother,
who knew of a yogi, Vishnu Bhaskar Lele,
and sent a telegram asking him to come.
Lele, when he received this telegram,
heard suddenly in a flash of intuition:
"Go to Baroda, you have to give initiation
to a very great soul."
So he came.
Lele wanted Sri Aurobindo to give up his political activities,
but this he refused.
He agreed, however, to suspend them for some time.
He disappeared suddenly from the tumultuous political scene.

Nirvana

For three days he stayed alone with Lele in a small room.
What happened in just three days' time?
    "Sit down", Lele told him, "look, and you will see that your
thoughts come into you from outside. Before they enter, fling
them back."

Sri Aurobindo narrates what followed:

"I had never heard before of thoughts coming visibly into the mind from outside, but I did not think either of questioning the truth or the possibility. I simply sat down and did it. In a moment my mind became silent as a windless air on a high mountain summit and then I saw one thought and then another coming in a concrete way from outside; I flung them away before they could enter... and in three days I was free."

"My mind became full of an eternal silence – it is still there."

There followed, he says, "a series of tremendously powerful experiences... they made me see with a stupendous intensity the world as a cinematographic play of vacant forms in the impersonal universality of the Absolute Brahman."

"What it brought was an inexpressible Peace, a stupendous silence, an infinity of release and freedom."

It was in this condition of the intense experience of the silent Brahman Consciousness that, a few days later, he went to Bombay. From the balcony of a friend's house he saw the myriad activities of the city,
its whole busy movement
as a picture in a cinema show,
all unreal and shadowy.
He describes this beautifully in his sonnet, *Nirvana*,
for indeed, this was the experience of Nirvana:

> The city, a shadow picture without tone,
> Floats, quivers unreal; forms without relief
> Flow, a cinema's vacant shapes...

Silence speaks

Now, another most moving experience came. While in that silent condition, he was invited by the Bombay National Union to address a meeting. How was he to deliver a speech

45

when the mind had become blank? Nor could he refuse, for he was so prominent and popular a leader. But Lele told him to accept, saying, all would be well.

He tells us what happened then:

"I asked Lele: 'What should I do?' He asked me to pray. But I was so absorbed in the Silent Brahman Consciousness that I could not pray. So I said to him that I was not in a mood to pray. Then he replied that it did not matter. He and others would pray and I had simply to go to the meeting and make Namaskar to the audience as Narayana, and then some voice would speak. I did exactly as he told me.... And all of a sudden something spoke."

It was a most stirring speech that he gave:

"Try to realise the strength within you, try to bring it forward, so that everything you do may be not your own doing but the doing of that Truth within you.... Because it is not you, it is something within you. What can all these tribunals, what can all the powers of the world do to that which is within you, that Immortal, that Unborn and Undying One, whom the sword cannot pierce, whom the fire cannot burn?..."

Divine Guide within

This realisation of the silent Brahman was so powerful that, as Sri Aurobindo says, finally Lele "was made by a Voice within him to hand me over to the Divine within me, enjoining an absolute surrender to His will..."

Lele felt that there was no need to give Sri Aurobindo any further instructions. He knew he could rely fully on the inner divine Guide within, he needed no human guru.

This absolute silence remained with him for ever.

But then, what about his work, you would ask?

46

Action in Yoga

Sri Aurobindo says,
"I had the realisation of Nirvana first,
then came the experience of action:
not my own, but from above....
"By this liberation one becomes free from the ego,
one becomes an instrument of the Divine Force....
"In the condition of absolute inner silence
I carried on a daily newspaper
and made a dozen speeches in the course of three or four
days..."
So he returned to full participation in political activity
once again.
For to him life became a field of the Divine,
God was the leader of the political awakening,
it was God who was working for the fulfilment of His
own purpose.
Sri Aurobindo felt that "something else than himself
took up his dynamic activity
and spoke and acted through him...."
He gave many powerful speeches all the way down from
Bombay to Calcutta, conducted many conferences in Bengal.

On April 30, 1908, at Muzzaffarpur, there was an attempt
to throw a bomb at the District Magistrate; but Sri Aurobindo
had no hand in it.
On May 1, several revolutionaries were arrested.

CHAPTER EIGHT

THE PILGRIMAGE OF ALIPORE

Early in the morning of May 2, while Sri Aurobindo was still
sleeping, the British Police charged up the stairs of his house,
revolvers in hand, and arrested him.

All over Bengal many young revolutionaries on whom the
police had been keeping an eye, were also arrested and jailed.
Their houses were searched; and one of them, afraid that the
party secret might leak out through him, shot himself.
The police searches and arrests continued.
Sri Aurobindo was taken to the police station
and thence to the Alipore Jail.
The trial began on May 19
and lasted nearly a full year.
There were 42 accused, 4,000 exhibits,
about 300 to 400 other "proofs",
222 witnesses!
Did you ever hear of such a prolonged affair?

Sri Aurobindo's sister, Sarojini, made an appeal "to the
public spirit and generosity of my countrymen" for his
defence; and from every corner of the country, rich and poor
sent their share,
for he was deeply loved for his self-sacrifice
and devotion to his Motherland.

Prison experiences

During his imprisonment Sri Aurobindo was at first lodged in
a solitary cell – nine feet by six, which served as bedroom,
dining-room and toilet all in one – but was afterwards
transferred to a huge room where he lived with the other
prisoners in the case.

However, after the assassination of the approver, all the

48

prisoners were confined in separate cells again, and met only in the court or at the daily exercises where they could not talk. Sri Aurobindo spent almost all his time
in reading the Gita and the Upanishads
and in intensive meditation.
He carried on his yoga
even when he had to live with others,
and accustomed himself to meditation
amid general talk and laughter, the playing of games and much noise and disturbance.

Sri Aurobindo himself has given us a glimpse into his first experience in jail:

"...I was taken... to Alipore and was placed in a solitary cell. There I waited day and night for the voice of God within me, to know what He had to say to me, to learn what I had to do... I remembered that a month or more before my arrest, a call had come to me to put aside all activity, to go into seclusion and look into myself... I... could not accept the call. My work was very dear to me.... He spoke to me again and said, 'The bonds you had not the strength to break, I have broken for you.... I had another thing for you to do and it is for that I have brought you here... to train you for my work.' "

But whilst he was waiting, he was in great physical and mental distress; then, Sri Aurobindo says,

"I called upon God with eagerness and intensity and prayed to him to prevent my loss of intelligence. That very moment there spread over my being such a gentle and cooling breeze, the heated brain became relaxed, easy and supremely blissful, such as in all my life I had never known before.... From that day all my troubles of prison life were over... that day in a single moment God had given my inner being such a strength that these sorrows... did not leave any trace or touch... It was possible to live happily during the long solitary confinement.... I also realised the extraordinary power and efficacy of prayer."*

* Translated from the original in Bengali.

49

"A prayer... can link man's strength to a transcendent Force."

It was in the courtyard of the Alipore jail, during the hours of walking, that a new and marvellous experience came.

God everywhere

"I looked at the jail... and it was no longer by the high walls that I was imprisoned; no, it was Vasudeva* who surrounded me. I walked under the branches of the tree in front of my cell but it was not the tree, I knew it was Vasudeva, it was Krishna whom I saw standing there and holding over me his shade. I looked at the bars of my cell, the very grating that did duty for a door and again I saw Vasudeva. It was Narayana* who was guarding and standing sentry over me..."

"Or I lay on the coarse blankets that were given me for a couch and felt the arms of Sri Krishna around me, the arms of my Friend and Lover.... I looked at the prisoners in the jail, the thieves, the murderers, the swindlers, and as I looked at them I saw Vasudeva, it was Narayana whom I found in these darkened souls and misused bodies."

In the Court too

Every day at the Sessions Court, in his iron cage,
it was the same experience:

"When the case opened... I was followed by the same insight... He said to me... 'Look now at the Magistrate, look now at the Prosecuting Counsel.' I looked and it was not the Magistrate whom I saw, it was Vasudeva, it was Narayana who was sitting there on the bench. I looked at the Prosecuting Counsel and it was not the Counsel... I saw, it was Sri Krishna who sat there and smiled. 'Now do you fear?' he said, 'I am in all men and I overrule their actions and their words.' "

* One of the names of God.

50

In the midst of the Court proceedings,
the whole day he remained absorbed in meditation,
hardly attending to the trial and the evidence.
He did not reply to the questions,
he listened only to the Voice within which repeated,

"I am guiding, therefore fear not. Turn to your own Work for which I have brought you to jail."

"Supernatural" Events

Several other strange and what are usually called "supernatural" experiences also came during that year in jail:

For a fortnight he heard constantly the voice of Vivekananda speaking to him in his meditation. It spoke on a special field of spiritual experience and then ceased.

Another "abnormal" experience was that of levitation.
He was deep in concentration, and asking himself:
"Are such *siddhis* possible?"
when he suddenly found himself raised up, half in mid-air, and the body remained suspended thus without any exertion on his part.

The jail warder had seen this happen,
and altogether dazzled, had spread the news everywhere,
so much so, that at one time all over India
people believed that Sri Aurobindo usually remained seated above the ground!

"...Day after day He showed me His wonders", says Sri Aurobindo,... things were opened to me which no material science could explain".

The Judgment Day

Yet, when his friend, C. R. Das, put aside his large practice and came to defend him, at first Sri Aurobindo felt it would be necessary to give him instructions. But once again a Voice within him said, "This is the man who will save you... put

51

aside those papers. It is not you who will instruct him. I will instruct him."

Then he left everything in God's hands, completely.

On the last day of the trial, May 5, 1909,
whilst everyone in the Court sat silent,
fearing the verdict of capital punishment,
suddenly C. R. Das burst into such inspired speech that judge, jury and the whole audience were swept off in its surge of power:

"...Long after the controversy will be hushed in silence, long after the turmoil, the agitation will have ceased, long after he is dead and gone, he will be looked upon as the poet of patriotism, as the prophet of nationalism and the lover of humanity.

"Long after he is dead and gone, his words will be echoed and re-echoed, not only in India, but across distant seas and lands. Therefore I say that the man in his position is not only standing before the bar of this Court, but before the bar of the High Court of History."

Was it not "the prophetic soul of the wide world dreaming on things to come" that spoke through his lips?

Sri Aurobindo was acquitted.

He heard over and over again the Voice within him:

"It is I who am doing this.... It is I who am doing this."

Uttarpara Speech

It was thus, after a full year in jail,
that Sri Aurobindo was released.
A few days later, on May 30, 1909
he gave his powerful historical speech at Uttarpara,
amidst great acclamation and honour and love.
Flower-garlands piled up in a huge heap,
nearly ten thousand men heard him
in pin-drop silence.
It was in this speech that he spoke of his experiences in prison.

52

After Alipore

All these experiences brought about a deep change in his view
of life: he had started Yoga to get spiritual strength for his
revolutionary work, but now the inner spiritual life and
realisation took him up entirely and his work became a part
and result of this as also it now exceeded the service and
liberation of India and fixed itself in an aim which was
world-wide in its bearing
and concerned the whole future of humanity.
For in the jail he had received the Divine Message:
    "I am raising up this nation to send forth my word....
            It is for the world and not for themselves
                    that they arise.
    I am giving them freedom for the service of the world."
During Sri Aurobindo's detention in jail
the political scene had changed completely.
Most of the Nationalist leaders were in prison or in exile,
the atmosphere was heavy with depression and discouragement.
Yet the feeling of revolt, though repressed,
was silently growing stronger, deeper.

The "Karmayogin"

Sri Aurobindo once again began his work,
determined to continue the struggle.
He gave many speeches – the first of these
    being his famous Uttarpara Speech,
attended political conferences
and started two weeklies,
the *Karmayogin* in English and *Dharma* in Bengali –
the *Karmayogin* carrying the significant motto of the Gita,
"Yoga is skill in works".
These journals had a very wide circulation.
Once again Sri Aurobindo proclaimed
the ideal of absolute independence

53

and advocated "no compromise", "no co-operation.
He would have nothing to do with the sham reforms
the Government proposed;
he declared them unreal and false and not acceptable.

"The Hammer of God"

Repression, then, was again in full swing:
imprisonments, accusations, arrests, deportations.
But Sri Aurobindo spoke to the people explaining the true place of repression and its significance in the political movement:

> "It is...a foolish idea...disproved over and over again in history, to think that a nation which has once risen, once has been called up by the voice of God to rise, will be stopped by mere physical repression.
>
> "...Repression is nothing but the hammer of God that is beating us into shape so that we may be moulded into a mighty nation and an instrument for His work in the world."

The Government was determined of course
to get rid of Sri Aurobindo again,
and this time decided to deport him.
"I was informed," he said humorously,
"that I was qualifying for deportation,"
his fault being that he appeared and spoke too much in public
meetings and wrote too much about freedom!
Friends urged him to leave British India and work from
outside,
but he did not think this was necessary.
He felt he could stop the Government's project
by writing a signed article in the *Karmayogin*,
"An Open Letter"
about his threatened deportation,
leaving to the country what he called
"My Last Will and Testament."

54

This served its purpose,
for the Government had to give up the idea of deporting him.
It had to wait for another excuse –
and it found an occasion when Sri Aurobindo wrote
another signed article reviewing the political situation.
One evening in February 1910,
at the *Karmayogin* office
he was warned of an approaching police search,
and his arrest.
Some of those present started preparing for a fight,
animated ideas were flying about,
when suddenly a distinct and well-known Voice from above
spoke three words:
"Go to Chandernagore".
He obeyed the command at once,
for now he acted only as moved by the divine guidance.
He did not consult anybody –
not even his colleagues.
Everything was done in the utmost silence and secrecy.
It was about eight o'clock when he started
and in about ten minutes he was at the river *ghat*,
having evaded the C.I.D. watchers of the office
(or were they not there that day?)
A common Ganges boat was hailed
and he was on his way
to Chandernagore
with his two young companions.

"I would hear, in my spirit's wideness solitary,
The Voice that speaks when mortal lips are mute".

CHAPTER NINE

CHANDERNAGORE

They reached Chandernagore
while it was yet dark.
He went there unannounced,
but a friend, Motilal Roy,
made secret arrangements for his stay and looked after his
needs.
Sri Aurobindo plunged entirely into solitary meditation,
and from that time ceased from all outer political activity.
He himself has told us why he did so:
    "I came away because...I got a very distinct *Adesh*.... I
    have cut my connection entirely with politics, but before I
    did so I knew from within that the work I had begun there
    was destined to be carried forward... that the ultimate
    triumph of the movement I had initiated was sure...."
Sri Aurobindo stayed in Chandernagore for nearly a month
and a half,
but the Government did not get
the faintest scent of it.
Even his co-workers
did not have the slightest idea
where he was.
He was in utter seclusion
and absorbed in *sadhana*.
Motilal Roy gives us a very simple impressionistic glimpse
into Sri Aurobindo's life at that period:
    "...A completely surrendered individual. One felt when he
    spoke as if somebody else were speaking through him. I
    placed the plate of food before him, – he simply gazed at it,
    then ate a little, just mechanically! He appeared to be
    absorbed even when he was eating; he used to meditate
    with open eyes, and see subtle forms and spiritual visions. '

56

New Plans

It was towards the end of March
that Sri Aurobindo received another command,
this time to go to Pondicherry –
Pondicherry, which he described later as
"my place of retreat, my cave of Tapasya, not of the ascetic
kind but a brand of my own."
Sri Aurobindo having asked Motilal Roy to make
arrangements for his departure, he wrote two letters,
one to Amar Chatterjee at Uttarpara,
the other to Sri Aurobindo's cousin, Sukumar Mitra
                                                    at Calcutta,
instructing them to meet Sri Aurobindo at the river *ghat*
and put him on board the *Dupleix*.
At the same time,
Sri Aurobindo's young friend, Suresh Chakravarty,
known familiarly as Moni,
also received a note
telling him to go to Pondicherry and arrange for
                                        Sri Aurobindo's stay there.
He was also given a letter of introduction
to one Srinivasachari,
who was connected with the revolutionary Tamil Weekly *India*
which supported the Nationalist policy.
The well-known Tamil poet, Subramaniam Bharati,
was also working with him.
This paper used to be published from Pondicherry.

   Moni, dressed as an Anglo-Indian to escape suspicion,
walked to Howrah station and left by train on March 28.
Sukumar Mitra saw him off and gave him Rs.30.
On the 31st he reached Pondicherry.

57

Moni in Pondicherry

Immediately he went to Srinivasachari
with the introductory letter,
asking him to make some arrangements for Sri Aurobindo
who was due to arrive on April 4.
But nobody would believe him.
They all suspected that he was a spy.
They felt that Sri Aurobindo would never choose
to come to Pondicherry,
so far from his field of work.
Moni begged and pleaded with them to take a house,
but they would not move.
The day of arrival came,
and Moni, much troubled within him,
went again to them:
"Sri Aurobindo is coming," he said,
"and you are not making any arrangements.
Where will he stay?"
They replied casually at first
that they would put him up when he came,
but secretly they had resolved
that should the news be false
and he not arrive that day,
they would give Moni a sound beating!
Then, perhaps to test him, they told Moni
they would give Sri Aurobindo a grand public reception
on his arrival.
But this upset Moni once again;
he argued much and persuaded them to drop the idea,
for Sri Aurobindo was coming secretly
and wanted to remain in seclusion.

The Journey

Let us now see what was happening at the other end. The

58

story of how Sri Aurobindo boarded the *Dupleix* is most thrilling, for, as we know, he had to come out of the safety of French Chandernagore, back to Calcutta, where he could be arrested at any moment.
The atmosphere in those days was most tense,
danger lurked in every corner.
Everything had to be done most cautiously and secretly.

Well, as we have seen, Sukumar Mitra got Motibabu's letter making him responsible for all the arrangements of the journey, and asking him to keep everything ready. Now, Sukumar was editor of the nationalist paper *Sanjivani*, and besides, Sri Aurobindo formerly used to stay in his house, so the C.I.D. police were constantly on the watch there. His task was hence doubly difficult.

Sukumar immediately set to work. He prepared two trunks (for Sri Aurobindo was to be accompanied by a friend, Bijoy Nag), called one of his nationalist workers, Nagendra Kumar Guha Roy, gave him these trunks and two names (real names taken from the list of *Sanjivani* subscribers, not imaginary ones, to guard against all police enquiries) and asked him to buy two second-class tickets for Colombo – yes, for Colombo, to mislead police investigations.
He was also told to reserve a double cabin.
Nagen, on seeing the trunks jokingly asked,
"Do they contain bombs?"
but was told not to bother about the contents,
but to keep quiet and do what work was given him.

Nagen bought the tickets and took the trunks with him. The next day, March 31, Sukumar asked him to hire a boat and take the trunks to the cabin of the *Dupleix*; he was asked also to wait with his boat for two passengers who would come from the other side of the river and whom he had to take to the steamer.
A little puzzled, Nagen asked how he would recognise the
two men.
Then suddenly it flashed upon him

59

that Sri Aurobindo must be the passenger.

"Is it not your Auro-da who is going?" he asked.

Sukumar smiled: "Yes, but how did you know?"

He admitted the truth, warning Nagen to be extremely cautious not to let it out.

As previously arranged Amar Chatterji met Sri Aurobindo at the *ghat* and ferried him across to the Calcutta-side of the Ganges,

but there was nobody there to meet them!

He hired a coach and took Sri Aurobindo to Sukumar's house, taking care, however, to stop the carriage at a distance and inquire. But Sukumar was not at home,

so they returned to the *ghat*.

Now, unfortunately, Nagen had been delayed in crossing the river and had missed Sri Aurobindo's boat. He returned and informed Sukumar, who told him to go back immediately and retrieve the trunks from the cabin.

It was already six o'clock in the evening when Nagen arrived. He found that the doctor who examined the passengers and issued health certificates had finished his work and gone home.

He took the Doctor's address from the Captain,

got back the trunks and put them in a hired carriage.

The coolie who carried the trunks,

hoping to get a good *bakshish*,

offered the information that he knew the Doctor's house and his servant too, and would manage everything.

Nagen, much relieved, asked the coolie to wait there for him and drove back to Sukumar's.

He found Sukumar anxiously awaiting him now;

he asked Nagen to hurry back to the *ghat*,

meet Sri Aurobindo

and arrange to get the Doctor's certificate.

So once again back he rushed,

and found Sri Aurobindo's carriage waiting by the wayside.

The coolie too was sitting there

and quickly informed him,
"Your Babu has come. I have told him about you.
It is very late already.
If we don't hurry the Doctor will go to sleep."
Nagen then had the trunks shifted to Sri Aurobindo's carriage
and got in himself.
The coolie climbed up to the coach-box,
and they drove to the Doctor's.
Bijoy Nag sat beside Sri Aurobindo;
he was to accompany him to Pondicherry.
The coolie spoke to the Doctor's servant
and the inspection was arranged.

But they had to wait for half an hour before the Doctor
called them in. There, on the verandah, while the young men
talked all the time, Sri Aurobindo sat utterly silent.
Strangely, the coolie having noticed this,
went and whispered to Nagen:
"Your big Babu seems frightened.
Perhaps he has never faced an English saheb and is afraid.
Please tell him the doctor is a good man,
there is no need to fear."
Nagen replied,
"No, the Babu is not afraid;
he was suffering from malarial fever and looks weak,
so you may have thought he is frightened."
But the coolie was not at all convinced!
He ran to Sri Aurobindo and said:
"Babuji, why are you afraid?
The Doctor is a very good man,
there is no reason to fear."
He caught Sri Aurobindo's arms and shook them a little.
The young men looked at each other at this strange
behaviour, and smiled.
Sri Aurobindo also smiled softly.
Within ten minutes the medical exam
was over and the certificate obtained,

61

but in that short time the Doctor remarked
that Sri Aurobindo spoke excellent English.

Back to the *ghat* then, they went, the young men still
anxious and worried as to how all would go off.
But on Sri Aurobindo's face there was not a trace
of anxiety or restlessness.
He sat unmoved, quiet,
almost like a statue –
as if in deep meditation.
It was nearly eleven o'clock
when they reached the *ghat*
and Sri Aurobindo and Bijoy Nag boarded the *Dupleix*.
Nagen touched Sri Aurobindo's feet and returned.
In the early hours of the next morning,
on April 1, 1910,
the steamer left Calcutta.

CHAPTER TEN

PONDICHERRY

April 4, 1910.
At 4 p.m. the *Dupleix* touched Pondicherry.
Sri Aurobindo had arrived.
Srinivasachari and Moni were at the port
to welcome him.
They took him to Shankar Chetty's house as his guest.
It is interesting to know
that in this very house
Swami Vivekananda had also stayed
during his tour of South India.
It was here that just about a week later
someone came to meet Sri Aurobindo
for a very special and important reason.
He wanted to meet a yogi,
for "he had been sent from France by Mira –
She whom we know as the Mother",
with a mission.
She had sent a sketch of a *yoga chakra* (a mystic symbol),
saying that its interpreter would be found in India
and that he would be her master and guide in yoga.
Sri Aurobindo gave the required interpretation.

As we shall see soon, the Mother who was then practising
her own yoga in France had, since a very long time, an inner
contact and communion with Sri Aurobindo. Only outwardly
they had not met or known each other.

"Uttar Yogi"

There was someone else also
who knew thus inwardly about Sri Aurobindo.
This was the famous yogi Nagai Japata,

63

who lived near Trichinapalli.
When on his death-bed he called his disciples around him,
among them a rich zamindar, K.V.R. Iyengar.
This man asked his master to whom he should go
for spiritual guidance in the future.
Nagai Japata remained silent for a while,
then said that a Mahayogi
would come from the North –
"Uttar Yogi" –
whose help he could take.
But as many yogis constantly went from North to South,
the disciple asked how he would recognise
this particular one.
Then the master gave two indications:
   i) he would come to the South seeking refuge,
   ii) he would be known by three sayings.
Now these three sayings
were the very three "madnesses"
that Sri Aurobindo had spoken about
in his letter to Mrinalini Devi.
This letter as you know, had been produced in the Court
during his trial and had thus been made public.
So both the clues fitted exactly
and Iyengar identified Sri Aurobindo
as the "Uttar Yogi",
and came seeking him.

  It was this Iyengar who published at his own cost the little
book *Yogic Sadhan* which Sri Aurobindo had "received"
while experimenting with automatic writing. He had not
really *written* the book himself and so later stopped its
circulation.

Life in Pondicherry – Hardships

Sri Aurobindo, with his young companions,
used to live in great hardship in these early years.

64

There was little or practically no money at all.

They lived in a small room with hardly any furniture, slept on the floor, Sri Aurobindo on a thin bedding, the others on straw mats.

There was very little to eat.

It was difficult even for his friends to send him money
as it was quite dangerous in those days for anyone
to help a revolutionary leader.

And Sri Aurobindo was watched and pestered by the British Indian police and C.I.D. men for years together, even in Pondicherry.

Indeed, the British Government could never believe that
                                                    Sri Aurobindo
had come to Pondicherry to practise his yoga in a quiet place.
They thought that yoga and religion were mere tricks,
tricks to hide revolutionary activities.

All that they really knew was that Sri Aurobindo
was "the most dangerous man in all India",
the one source of all their troubles,
the brain behind the whole Independence Movement.

Therefore they suspected that
revolutionary instructions and plans,
perhaps even bombs and pistols,
were being supplied by him
from Pondicherry.

And so it was that secret police agents
constantly haunted his house,
kept watch on every movement, noted his visitors
and made all sorts of attempts
to get rid of him.

"Spy Stories"
Conspiracy No. 1

There are at least three "spy-stories" of these early days.
The British Government had set its spies everywhere:

65

in Madras, on the roads to Pondicherry
and in the town –
plain clothes men of the C.I.D.
Pondicherry in those days was full of local *goondas* too,
and specially during the political election campaigns
anarchy reigned in the place:
there was rioting and murder,
blood flowed freely.
It was during such a campaign
that the British tried one of their worst moves.

The spies conspired with a local political leader who was
influential and had some of these *goondas* in his pay, to carry
off Sri Aurobindo from the limits of French India, so that he
could be immediately arrested by the British on some
trumped-up charge.
Sri Aurobindo's young comrades-in-arms
got wind of this plan,
and arming themselves with acid bottles
sat up the whole night
to "welcome" the kidnappers!
But... nobody came.
What had stopped them?
Most strangely, on that very day,
against this very leader,
a warrant of arrest had been issued
by the opposite political party,
and it was he who had to run away
from Pondicherry to Madras.
How marvellous are the ways of Providence!

Conspiracy No. 2

Of course, the British police,
though foiled in this attempt,
could not sit in peace,
for every day more and more revolutionaries

66

were crossing over to French India as refugees.
The C.I.D. tried another plan:
they forged documents, collected photographs,
and maps and charts and some letters,
packed them in a tin
and secretly threw them into a well
in the house of one of the revolutionaries,
Aiyer, who was a good friend of Sri Aurobindo's.
They wanted to implicate the whole group
and show that all of them were engaged
in dangerous activities.
However, as these British agents
could not act openly in French territory,
they engaged a Pondicherry man, one Mayuresan,
to inform the French police
that if the houses of these revolutionaries were searched,
proofs of their conspiracies would be found.
Once again, see what happened.
The maid-servant at Aiyar's, drawing water from the well,
brought up the tin!
On Sri Aurobindo's advice,
the French police were immediately informed.
They came and found in the tin
seditious pamphlets and papers,
some with an image of Kali,
some written in Bengali.
The idea was to show that these refugees
were carrying on secret correspondence
with revolutionaries abroad
and conspiring against the British Government.

As all the houses were to be searched,
the investigating French Magistrate
came to Sri Aurobindo's room also.
The room was almost bare:

a few trunks, a table and a chair.
In the table drawers he found books and papers
on some of which Greek was written.
He was so surprised, he could only exclaim:
"He knows Greek! He knows Latin!"
And filled with admiration for this scholar-yogi
he removed his men and went away.
The informer, Mayuresan,
strongly threatened for making a false complaint,
disappeared from Pondicherry.

As a matter of fact, the French Government had been quite
good to all these political refugees, shielding them as a point
of honour. But the British Government started putting much
pressure on them to deport these revolutionaries or to hand
them over. A proposal was made then to take them to Algiers.
Sri Aurobindo's friends, the Tamil Nationalist leaders, among
them the poet-patriot Bharati, came to him in much excite-
ment to ask whether he would not prefer to leave India. Sri
Aurobindo sat silent for a minute or two, then quietly replied,
"Mr. Bharati, I am not going to budge an inch from here!"
The others accepted the decision and dropped the idea of
going.

Conspiracy No. 3

The two main 'conspiracies' of the C.I.D. had failed.
But they did not give up looking for proofs,
making false reports,
gathering imaginary 'seditious' stories.
One day, Sri Aurobindo's young companions were utterly
stunned by a most unforeseen event.
About six or eight months earlier, Bijoy Nag's cousin who was
suffering from T.B. had come to Pondicherry for a change of
air, also hoping that Sri Aurobindo would cure him by yogic
power.

68

With him had come a companion and servant, Biren Roy,
who, being a Bengali, soon became the general manager,
cook, etc. of Sri Aurobindo's house and later almost a
member of the household.
Now, suddenly, one day,
this Biren had his head completely shaved.
And seeing him, Moni,
though usually very fashionable
and particular about his looks,
also took a fancy for a complete shave.
Biren tried to persuade him to give up the idea,
but Moni was insistent and obstinate.
A day or two later,
late in the evening at about 10 o'clock,
all the inmates were sitting around Sri Aurobindo,
when there occurred a regular scene!
Biren suddenly stood up and shouted,
"Do you know who I am?
I am a spy, a C.I.D. man!
I can't keep it to myself any longer.
I must speak out, I must confess...."
With this he fell at Sri Aurobindo's feet.
Everyone was dumbfounded.
Could this be true? Was this a joke?
They started laughing.
But Biren thought they knew everything
and were fooling him.
He jumped up, went to the next room,
and brought Rs.50 from his trunk.
"See, here is the proof.
Where could I have got all this money?
This is the reward of my evil deed.
Never, never will I do this work again.
I give you my word, I ask your forgiveness...."
All sat silent and still.
They did not know what to think or say.

69

This is how it had come about.
Biren had shaved his head
so that the police spies might spot him as their man
from the rest of the young Bengalis.
But when Moni too shaved his head,
Biren suspected that he,
or perhaps all of them,
had found out his secret
and that Moni had shaved his head deliberately.
So partly out of fear,
partly out of true repentance,
(but really due to some deeper pressure),
he confessed.

After this incident
the atmosphere in the house
became quite serious and disturbed.
All were worried.
How could this have happened?
A spy living in their very midst?
Bijoy was so furious
he would have done something drastic.
However, soon Biren left,
and afraid of the revolutionaries' vengeance,
went off to Mesopotamia.
But the tension in the air remained for a long time.
Suspicion walked through the roads.
A large number of secret police agents
still lurked in the town.
Biren's confession was indeed a miracle.

70

1914
The Mother's Coming

March 29, 1914.
3.30 p.m.
The Mother met Sri Aurobindo for the first time.
But she had known him for years in her spiritual experiences,
and indeed, this was why she came from France
to work with him.
Speaking of this, in answer to a question
about her mission on earth,
Mother said:

"Between eleven and thirteen a series of psychic and
spiritual experiences revealed to me not only the existence of
God but man's possibility of meeting with Him or revealing
Him integrally in consciousness and action, of manifesting
Him upon earth in a life divine. This, along with a practical
discipline for its fulfilment, was given to me, during my body's
sleep, by several teachers some of whom I met afterwards on
the physical plane. Later on, as the interior and exterior
development proceeded, the spiritual and psychic relation
with one of these beings became more and more clear.... I was
led to call him Krishna and henceforth I was aware that it was
with him (whom I should meet on earth one day) that the
divine work had to be done....

"The moment I saw Sri Aurobindo I recognised him as the
being I used to call Krishna... this is enough to explain why I
am fully convinced that my place and work are near him in
India."

The day after this first meeting, on March 30,
Mother wrote in her 'Meditations':
"It matters not if there are hundreds of beings
plunged in the deepest ignorance.
He whom we saw yesterday is here on earth.
His presence is enough to prove that a day shall come

71

when darkness shall be transformed into Light
when Thy reign shall be indeed established upon earth."

The Arya

About this time, Paul Richard, a French thinker and scholar,
persuaded Sri Aurobindo to start a philosophical journal to
give the world his vision and knowledge in terms of the
intellect.
It was thus that the *Arya, A Philosophical Review*,
was started on August 15, 1914,
Sri Aurobindo's forty-second birthday.
Between 1914 and 1920, in one vast sweep, non-stop,
Sri Aurobindo wrote almost the whole of his work,
nearly five thousand pages,
and most strangely,
not one book after another,
but four, five, even six books serialised at a time!
A few months later, Richard was called back to France
as the First World War had broken out,
and so Sri Aurobindo was left alone
to write 64 pages of philosophy every month!
Quietly, undisturbed,
he went on writing.
He said he could manage it, because
   "it is out of a silent mind that I write whatever
   comes ready-shaped from above."
Sri Aurobindo's main works –
all, except his great epic, *Savitri* –
were first written for the *Arya*.
Many of these embodied the inner knowledge that had come
to him in his practice of Yoga; others were concerned with
the spirit and significance of Indian civilisation and culture,
the true meaning of the Vedas,
the progress of human society,
the nature and evolution of poetry,

72

the possibility of the unification of the human race.
They are all there now in book-form for you to read in the
future according to your interests.*

On February 21, 1915
the Mother's birthday was celebrated
for the first time in Pondicherry.
On February 22, the Mother went back to France.
In the years 1915 and 1916
Sri Aurobindo and the Mother wrote several letters
which describe their common mission,
their spiritual experiences,
the trials they were facing in their work for humanity
and their unshakable faith
in the ultimate victory.

* *The Life Divine, The Synthesis of Yoga, The Human Cycle, The Ideal of Human Unity, Essays on the Gita, The Future Poetry, The Secret of the Veda, The Foundations of Indian Culture, The Isha Upanishad.*

CHAPTER ELEVEN

INTENSE SADHANA

The Mother returned to Pondicherry
on April 24, 1920
to stay there permanently now,
and join Sri Aurobindo in his work and sadhana.
Never, since then, has the Mother gone out of Pondicherry
again.
Between 1920 and 1926
the sadhana became extremely intense and deep.
Sri Aurobindo saw that the magnitude of the spiritual work
set before him needed the concentration of all his energies.
Years of inner striving and intense Yoga
were required for him to find a real way
and trace it out completely.
"But the sadhana and the work were waiting
for the Mother's coming".

So far, Sri Aurobindo had taken no disciples. He lived in
retirement with a few companions of his political days, with
whom he had the relation of friends, not of Guru and
disciples.
Afterwards, there was a gradual development of spiritual
relations,
and when the Mother came back
more people began to come to follow the spiritual path.
It was thus that a community of sadhaks was formed
for the maintenance and guidance of those
who had left everything behind
for the sake of a higher life.
The Mother gradually took charge of the whole management:
arrangements had to be made for lodging,
for the service of food,
for decent living and hygiene.

74

All these activities grew of themselves as the needs arose,
and slowly led to the foundation
of the Ashram in November 1926.

November 24, 1926

From the beginning of 1926
the work of guiding the disciples
began to move towards the Mother.
It seemed as though Sri Aurobindo
was slowly withdrawing into seclusion,
and the Mother taking up the great work
both of inner sadhana and of outer organisation.
The daily meditations
became more and more concentrated and intense.
Something seemed to be about to happen,
a feeling grew in all the disciples
that some Higher Power would descend.
Sri Aurobindo himself had been working intensively
and for a long time preparing this descent.
At last, on November 24, 1926
this Higher Power descended.
The Mother called this day the Day of Victory,
for this descent marked
a great step in Sri Aurobindo's work.

Sri Aurobindo calls this Power the "Overmind".
He speaks of a still higher power, the "Supermind",
which he also wanted to bring,
and brought down, on earth.
It is difficult for us to understand these Powers,
but Sri Aurobindo's explanation may help us a little.
He says, "By the Supermind is meant
the full Truth-Consciousness of the Divine....
Between the Supermind and the human mind
are a number of ranges, planes....

75

The Overmind is the highest of these ranges;
it is full of lights and powers...."
He said, "The Overmind has to be reached and brought down
before the supermind descent is at all possible –
for the Overmind is the passage...."
No doubt, we cannot grasp these things,
for the ordinary mind is very limited.
Of this higher power, Sri Aurobindo says in *Savitri*,

> There is a Consciousness mind cannot touch,
> Its speech cannot utter nor its thought reveal.

On this day another phase
in Sri Aurobindo's mighty spiritual work began.
On this day too, Sri Aurobindo retired
into complete solitude.
And it was then that
"Sri Aurobindo Ashram"
was officially founded,
under the Mother's direction and guidance.

Retirement and work

Yet, in his retirement Sri Aurobindo kept a close watch
on all that was happening in the world and in India
and actively intervened whenever necessary.
He shared, too, the Mother's work of guiding the disciples,
mainly by writing letters,
packed with inner help and power,
explaining their difficulties, their experiences,
directing them, giving them knowledge.
In one of these letters answering a disciple's complaint for
delay, he says,

> "You do not realise that I have to spend 12 hours over the
> ordinary correspondence, numerous reports, etc. I work 3
> hours in the afternoon and the whole night up to 6 in the
> morning over this."

76

Hundreds of these letters have now been published. They make three large volumes in the Centenary edition of Sri Aurobindo's works. Here is a small selection for you of a few of the shortest and simplest.

In one he explains the different shades of meaning of words often used as synonyms:

"Faith is a feeling in the whole being, belief is mental, confidence means trust in a person or in the Divine or a feeling of surety about the result of one's seeking or endeavour."

And in another he gives guidance to one in difficulty and a sure method of knowing what is good for us:

"In moments of trial, faith in the divine protection and the call for that protection; at all times the faith that what the Divine wills is the best.

"It is what turns you towards the Divine that must be accepted as good for you – all is bad for you that turns you away from the Divine."

In another yet he says:

"Prayers should be full of confidence, without sorrow or lamenting."

One of the loveliest is this single-sentence letter which says so much:

"A sincere heart is worth all the extraordinary powers in the world."

In some he gives simple directions for our inner progress and character-building:

"To be able to be regular is a great force, one becomes master of one's time and one's movements."

"Only those who sympathise can help – surely also one should be able to see the faults of others without hatred. Hatred injures both parties, it helps none."

And this penetrating, deep affirmation:

"Sacrifice depends on the inner attitude. If one has nothing outward to sacrifice, one has always oneself to give."

There are lots of humorous, extremely witty letters too. For he was a great humorist. This is what he said about humour:

77

"Sense of humour? It is the salt of existence. Without it the world would have got utterly out of balance – it is unbalanced enough already – and rushed to blazes long ago."

And here's a last one to chisel in our hearts for a life-time:

"Remain firm through the darkness; the light is there and will conquer."

Sri Aurobindo also gave "Darshan" in public four times a year. When asked, however, why he had retired from outer activity, he said that he had to keep himself out from the type of work which Mother was doing in order to find time for "his real work".

What, then, was this: his real Work?

CHAPTER TWELVE

HIS WORK AND YOGA

In order to understand what Sri Aurobindo meant
by "my real work",
we must try to know something about his Yoga.
Now, "What is Yoga"? you may ask.
"Yoga" simply means "union" –
the union of the human soul with the Divine,
the union of man with God.
All the paths, the ways and practices which lead to this union
are called paths of yoga.
Sri Aurobindo tells us what the aim of his yoga is:
  "It is the object of my Yoga to transform life
  by bringing down into it
  the Light, Power and Bliss of the divine Truth...."
  The final aim is to create a divine life on this earth and in the
earthly existence. Sri Aurobindo did not teach an escape from
life or mere *sannyasa*.
He wanted Life to be "a flame-discovery of God",
the world to "manifest the unveiled Divine".

  Sri Aurobindo says, "We are here to do what the Divine
wills and to create a world in which the Divine Will can
manifest its truth.... Our yoga is not for our own sake but for
the sake of the Divine."

  And again, "The object of the Yoga is... to love the Divine
for the Divine's sake alone, to be tuned in our nature into the
nature of the Divine, and in our will and works and life to be
the instrument of the Divine....
Its object is not to be a great yogi or a Superman....
The Divine alone is our object."
But some of you may ask,
"What or Who is the Divine?"
Sri Aurobindo, like all the ancient sages of India, tells us

79

that behind the appearances of the universe
there is a Reality,
a Self of all things,
one and eternal.
This is "the Divine".
All beings are united in that One Self and Spirit,
but are ignorant of their true Self and Reality
because of a veil of separation in their nature.
By Yoga this veil can be removed
and man can become aware of his true Self,
the Divinity within us and all things.

Evolution

Our world, Sri Aurobindo teaches, is the scene
of an ascending evolution,
which goes from the stone to the plant,
from the plant to the animal,
from the animal to man.
Man, for the moment, seems to be at the summit,
so he believes that there is nothing on earth superior to him.
But surely he is mistaken,
for in his physical nature he is still almost wholly an animal,
a thinking and speaking animal,
but yet an animal in his habits and instincts.
The next step of the evolution, then, must be taken:
the animal man must become the divine man,
he must develop a new higher spiritual consciousness.
(which Sri Aurobindo called the Supermind or the
                                        Supramental),
the Truth-Consciousness,
and live a new life, perfectly harmonious,
good and beautiful,
happy and fully conscious.
"During the whole of his life upon earth", says the Mother,
"Sri Aurobindo gave all his time to establish in himself this

80

consciousness... and to help those gathered around him to
realise it."
This, then, was his main work:
to bring down this great Power to transform the earth-life
and to show others the path to a new divine life
upon a new earth.
It is to this path and to this life
that the Mother calls all the brave little children of the world –
to Truth's final victory.
This is the path of the Integral (*Purna*) Yoga:
to realise the Divine,
to approach Him with love and devotion and *bhakti*,
to serve Him with one's works
and to know Him –
finally, to surrender all our nature to Him
that it may be transformed and made divine
by the Light of Truth.

From November 1938 Sri Aurobindo found it necessary to
change the course of his work, for the looming world-crisis
needed a deeper concentration all the time.

Sri Aurobindo saw, too, that the main movement of the
inner spiritual work needed an equal concentration.

The Inner War

For, from the seclusion and solitude of his room
he was waging a terrible spiritual battle
with the Forces of Darkness, the dark Asuric forces,
which oppose the coming of the Truth-Light.
He had to plunge deep, into the darkest Abyss
of unconsciousness and falsehood,
into the utter Night,
the storm and chaos and tumult,
he had to fight a grim fierce battle
before the Truth could be completely established here

81

and the earth uplifted out of its darkness
towards the Divine.
All his work was undertaken to bring
    Light and Truth and Peace and Joy
      to earth and men.

      In me the spirit of immortal Love
      Stretches its arms out to embrace mankind.

And it was because of his deep love for men that he took upon
himself this terrible burden.
    He says, "It is only divine Love which can bear the burden I
have to bear, that all have to bear who have sacrificed
everything else to the one aim of uplifting earth out of its
darkness towards the Divine."
In a very beautiful poem of his, Sri Aurobindo speaks
of this work in "The Abyss":

      I have been digging deep and long
        Mid a horror of filth and mire,
      A bed for the golden river's song,
        A home for the deathless fire.

And the battle is a very real battle:

      My gaping wounds are a thousand and one,

he says, and again,

      I have laboured and suffered in Matter's night
        To bring the fire to man.

But not only do the dark forces struggle against the Truth,
the whole earth resists
and man himself.

82

The Truth of truths men fear and deny,
The Light of lights they refuse...

And so, "each battle has to be fought and refought", he says.
But not only did Sri Aurobindo wage this spiritual war
secretly, he also used his force in a constant action upon the
world forces.
When, for instance, during the Second World War
he saw that behind Hitler and Nazism
there were dark Asuric forces,
and that if they were victorious
all mankind would be enslaved to the tyranny of evil
and the spiritual evolution of man suffer a set-back,
he actively intervened,
just at the critical moment of Dunkirk,
and the whole tide of war turned
in favour of the Allies.
   So, too, he intervened with his spiritual force against the
Japanese aggression when it became evident that Japan
intended to attack and even invade and conquer India. And
once again the tide of Japanese victory changed immediately
into a rapid, crushing and overwhelming defeat.

This spiritual dynamic power which many yogis hold
   is greater than any other force and more effective.
It was this power, also, that Sri Aurobindo put
into the movement of India's liberation,
and indeed, it was
not a coincidence or a chance accident
but "the sanction and seal of the Divine Force"
upon his work,
         that India declared herself free
            on August 15, 1947.
         It was Sri Aurobindo's birthday.

August 15, 1947

The message he gave for this day is so heart-stirring,
so charged with words of destiny,
that you must hear it:
"August 15th, 1947 is the birthday of free India.
It marks for her the end of an old era, the beginning of a new
age. But we can also make it by our life and acts as a free
nation an important date in a new age opening for the whole
world, for the political, social, cultural and spiritual future of
humanity.

"August 15th is my own birthday and it is naturally
gratifying to me that it should have assumed this vast significance.... Indeed, on this day I can watch almost all the
world-movements which I had hoped to see fulfilled in my
life-time, though then they looked like impracticable dreams,
arriving at fruition or on their way to achievement. In all these
movements free India may well play a large part and take a
leading position.

"The first of these dreams was a revolutionary movement
which would create a free and united India. India today is free
but she has not achieved unity.... The old communal division
into Hindus and Muslims seems now to have hardened into a
permanent political division of the country*.... If it lasts,
India may be seriously weakened, even crippled: civil strife
may always remain possible, possible even a new invasion and
foreign conquest. India's internal development and prosperity
may be impeded... her destiny impaired.... This must not be;
the partition must go; unity must and will be achieved, for it is
necessary for the greatness of India's future.

"Another dream was for the resurgence and liberation of
the peoples of Asia and her return to her great role in the
progress of human civilisation.... There India has her part to
play and has begun to play it with an energy and ability which

* Sri Aurobindo is referring here to the division of India into "India"
and "Pakistan".

84

already indicate the measure of her possibilities and the place she can take in the council of the nations.

"The third dream was a world-union forming the outer basis of a fairer, brighter and nobler life for all mankind.... That unification of the human world is under way.... Here too, India has begun to play a prominent part.... A new spirit of oneness will take hold of the human race.

"Another dream, the spiritual gift of India to the world has already begun.... Amid the disasters of the time more and more eyes are turning towards her with hope and there is even an increasing resort not only to her teachings, but to her psychic and spiritual practice.

"The final dream was a step in evolution which would raise man to a higher and larger consciousness.... This evolution... since it must proceed through a growth of the spirit... the initiative can come from India and... the central movement may be hers.

"Such is the content which I put into this date of India's liberation...."*
Do we not hear once again
the Voice of Krishna which spoke in the jail:
    "I am raising up this nation to send forth my word...
            it is for the world... that they arise....
    I am giving them freedom for the service of the world."

The Poetical Works

Sri Aurobindo once said, "I was a poet and a politician, not a philosopher."
Yet the whole world knows him first as a yogi and a
                                        philosopher,
and students of Indian History know him as a politician,
but not many know him as a poet.

* As the reader will see, this Message has been slightly shortened. Those who are interested should read the full message in *Sri Aurobindo on Himself* (Centenary Volume 26, p. 400).

We too have so far seen
first, Sri Aurobindo in the field of politics,
then, Sri Aurobindo's Yoga and philosophy.
Only in passing did we get a glimpse of him
writing a little poetry in England and then at Baroda.
But he is as great as a poet, and has given the world
the greatest poem of all time,
his magnificent epic, *Savitri*.
Poetry Sri Aurobindo wrote right through his life;
indeed till the very end.
His early lyrical verse is very beautiful with wonderful touches
of deep insight everywhere.
During the Baroda period, he wrote his long narrative poems
Love and Death and *Urvasie*,
and many poetic dramas too.
The conquest of Death by Love, the theme of this early poem,
is also, on a different level,
the theme of *Savitri*
and, as we saw, the first version of *Savitri* belongs to this
very period.
During his political period too
he wrote many, many poems and plays,
some of which were published in his political journals.
You should all read the story of Baji Prabhou,
the great hero, Shivaji's warrior-friend,
of his fearless courage and noble self-sacrifice, –
for he knew that man derives all his strength from the Divine.
But of course, Sri Aurobindo's finest poetical work
belongs to the Pondicherry period.
He says of his philosophical writings:
   "Everything I wrote came from Yogic experience,
   knowledge and inspiration,"
and he continues, "So too my greater power over poetry and
perfect expression was acquired... from the heightening of my
consciousness...."
The most lovely lyrics,

Sri Aurobindo writing for the 'Arya', 1918-20

Sri Aurobindo, 1950

the most powerful sonnets,
the miraculous hexameter epic *Ilion*,
narrative poems and lyrics in quantitative and new metres,
all are crowded into this period,
– almost all of them
poems of deep spiritual experience....

"Savitri"

– And finally, the crown of all his works,
the marvellous epic *Savitri*,
an epic of over 23,800 lines,
which he wrote and re-wrote through the years,
polished and perfected,
to embody his vast vision of Truth,
his spiritual vision of the universe and of Life,
his vision of the future,
when the world
would "manifest the unveiled Divine".
All his spiritual knowledge is there,
the intimate knowledge and experience
of all the planes of existence,
from the darkest depths to the supreme Heights,
the shining worlds of Truth.
We could call him in his own words
"a poet of the cosmic mysteries".

Savitri is *A Legend and a Symbol*,
so the outer story carries deep significances,
everything has a vaster, deeper meaning.
The story, based upon the *Mahabharata* legend,
tells of Savitri, "the Divine Word, daughter of the Sun,*
goddess of the supreme Truth who comes down"

* "Savitur", the Sun, the symbol of the Supermind or Truth-
Consciousness.

to save Satyavan, "the soul... descended
into the grip of death and ignorance."
It is so that Savitri, the incarnation of the Divine Mother
in Sri Aurobindo's poem, asks of the Lord this final boon:

> Thy embrace which rends the living knot of pain,
> Thy joy, O Lord, in which all creatures breathe,
> Thy magic flowing waters of deep love,
> Thy sweetness give to me for earth and men.

And she is promised that when all her work is done,
a new power will wake in man:

> The Eternal's truth shall mould his thoughts and acts,
> The Eternal's truth shall be his light and guide.
> All then shall change, a magic order come...
> A divine harmony shall be earth's law,
> Beauty and Joy remould her way to live...
> Nature shall live to manifest secret God...
> This earthly life become the life divine.

These are some of the lines
which express Sri Aurobindo's vision of the future.
The Mother says of *Savitri*:
"Its revelation is prophetic."
It is "intuitive, revealing poetry"
and its language is
"the inspired, inevitable Word",
the revelatory speech of the *Mantra*.
Sri Aurobindo had been working on *Savitri* for years,
                                              as we saw,
revising and re-casting it,
expanding and perfecting it
in his lordly, leisurely way.
One day, in September 1950, he told his disciple-scribe:
"I must finish *Savitri* soon."
This seemed a most unusual statement from him
who ever moved in an unhurrying, unperturbed pace.

88

Mahasamadhi

It was only on December 5, 1950
that these strange words found a meaning.
On this day in the early hours,
the Master withdrew from his body.
That he took a decision to do so is certain,
for like all great Yogis he was master of death.
They "die at will", as we Indians say,
theirs is *icchamrityu.*
It was a willed, deliberate withdrawal,
and on its mystery only the Mother, who knows all,
has thrown some light:
"Our Lord has sacrificed himself totally for us.... He was not
compelled to leave his body, he chose to do so for reasons so
sublime that they are beyond the reach of human mentality..."
Perhaps we have, in a way, his own 'explanation' in *Savitri*:

> He must pass to the other shore of falsehood's sea,
> He must enter the world's dark to bring there light...
> He must enter the eternity of Night
> And know God's darkness as He knows his Sun,
> For this he must go down into the pit,
> For this he must invade the dolorous Vasts...
> Then shall be ended here the Law of Pain.

The Mother also said, "He has sacrificed his physical life in
order to help more fully his work of transformation."

His shining, majestic body lay in state – as thousands of
people passed by having his last Darshan – for more than four
days; it remained perfectly unchanged, for, as the Mother
explained, it was charged with a deep concentration of
Supramental Light.

On December 9, at 5 p.m., the body was laid in the vault
prepared in the centre of the Ashram courtyard.
The Lord had indeed come down into our midst.
It seemed as though through and in his body
this Light had entered the very heart of the Earth,
the heart of Matter,
that he had come down

"Bringing the fires of the splendour of God
Into the human abyss."

Now he seemed to be with the world more than ever before.
The Mother said on the 7th of December:

"Lord, Thou hast given me the assurance that Thou
wouldst stay with us until Thy work is achieved… until earth is
transformed."

And Mother wrote too the beautiful thanksgiving
and prayer which is engraved upon his Samadhi:

"To Thee who hast been the material envelope of our
Master, to Thee our infinite gratitude. Before Thee who
hast done so much for us, who hast worked, struggled,
suffered, hoped, endured so much, before Thee who hast
willed all, attempted all, prepared, achieved all for us,
before Thee we bow down and implore that we may never
forget, even for a moment, all we owe to Thee."

May the Lord grant "that we may be worthy
of this marvellous Presence,"
"that everything in us… be more and more consecrated to the
fulfilment of his work."

With this last magnificent self-giving,
Sri Aurobindo seems to have achieved his purpose:

The gulf twixt the depths and the heights is bridged
And the golden waters pour

90

Down the sapphire mountain rainbow-ridged
And glimmer from shore to shore.

Heaven's fire is lit in the breast of the earth
And the undying suns here burn...

He has released the Light and Force needed for the manifesta-
tion of a new world.
"What Sri Aurobindo represents in the world's history is not a
teaching, not even a revelation,
                    it is a decisive action
                    direct from the Supreme,"
                    says the Mother.

The Ashram

And so naturally his work continues –
not only continues but grows vaster, richer every day.
The Mother is its inspirer, director, guide.
If we turn back our eyes a moment to that day in 1926
when the Ashram was founded
with merely twenty-four *sadhakas*,
and see how through these years it has grown
into a large community
of nearly two thousand people,
we shall understand something of the force behind it.
There are people there of all types and 'traditions',
of various nationalities, of all ages and social classes,
aspirants and seekers from all over the world.
Yes, of all types,
for the Ashram, as Sri Aurobindo once said,
is a vast 'laboratory',
a field of experiment,
where all the basic difficulties of human nature,
all the problems of human life,

91

are faced and conquered.
Every kind of work is done, all the professions are
                                        represented;
for whatever the work, when dedicated to the Divine
it becomes the means
of self-discovery,
of self-realisation,
of uniting with the Truth of one's being,
of attaining the integrally perfect life in the Spirit.

"To know the highest Truth and to be in harmony with it is the condition of right being, to express it in all that we are, experience and do is the condition of right living", says Sri Aurobindo.

International Centre of Education

In 1951, "with the purpose of realising one of
Sri Aurobindo's most cherished ideals,"
the Mother founded
the *Sri Aurobindo International Centre of Education.*
   She declared that Sri Aurobindo had considered the formation of such a centre "as one of the best means of preparing the future humanity to receive the supramental light that will transform the élite of today into a new race manifesting upon earth the new light and force and life."
   The Centre follows Sri Aurobindo's principles of teaching and works on lines laid down by him and the Mother.

Hundreds of students from all over the world
study here, shaping in their progress
the cultural and spiritual unity of mankind,
creating the basis of the new world.

92

Auroville

As the beginning of this new creation,
years ago the Mother had foreseen
a model township,
a symbol of human unity
and world-brotherhood.
On February 28, 1968 the Mother inaugurated this new city,
         AUROVILLE
         the City of Dawn,
         the City of Sri Aurobindo.
In its foundation urn is mixed the soil of about a hundred and
twenty countries of the world and the soil of Sri Aurobindo
Ashram and the soil of Auroville.
Its Charter lays down one condition:

"To live in it one must be a willing servitor
of the Divine Consciousness."

This is but one centre of the radiation
of Sri Aurobindo's power and world-vision.

Now, all the world over Centres have been started
for the teaching and practice of Sri Aurobindo's Yoga.
         The New Age of the Spirit
         dawns upon the earth,
         it is the rebirth of India,
         the rebirth of the world.
It is the "decisive action direct from the Supreme"
         in the world's history,
         which Sri Aurobindo represents.
"And the things that were promised are fulfilled."

         "I saw the Omnipotent's flaming pioneers
         Over the heavenly verge which turns towards life
         Come crowding down the amber stairs of birth;

93

Forerunners of a divine multitude
Out of the paths of the morning star they came...
I saw them cross the twilight of an age,
The sun-eyed children of a marvellous dawn...
The architects of immortality."

To these "sun-eyed children of a marvellous dawn,"
these "radiant children of Paradise"
who come
"clarioning darkness' end"
this little book is addressed.

There is a truth to know, a work to do....

All is too little that the world can give:
Its power and knowledge are the gifts of Time
And cannot fill the spirit's sacred thirst....

There is a need within the soul of man
The splendours of the surface never sate....

We are pilgrims of the everlasting Truth.
We make our daily way a pilgrimage.
In our journey through life
Sri Aurobindo's voice directs us:

Lean for thy soul's support on Heaven's strength,
Turn towards high Truth, aspire to love and peace....*

and Mother gives us a beautiful prayer:
"Make of us the hero warriors we aspire to become.
May we fight successfully
the great battle of the future that is to be born
against the past that seeks to endure;
so that the new things may manifest
and we be ready to receive them."

* Most of the lines on this page are from Sri Aurobindo's poetry.